REMEMBERING AMERICA

# Remembering America

## How We Have Told Our Past

LAWRENCE R. SAMUEL

UNIVERSITY OF NEBRASKA PRESS
*Lincoln and London*

Library of Congress Cataloging-in-Publication
Data
Samuel, Lawrence R.
Remembering America: how we have told our past /
Lawrence R. Samuel.
pages cm
Includes bibliographical references.
ISBN 978-0-8032-5433-6 (cloth: alk. paper)
ISBN 978-0-8032-8083-0 (epub)
ISBN 978-0-8032-8084-7 (mobi)
ISBN 978-0-8032-8085-4 (pdf)
1. Historiography—United States—History—20th
century.    2. United States—Historiography.
3. Historians—United States—History—20th
century.    I. Title.
E175.S27 2015
973.072—dc23
2015002787

Set in Minion by Westchester Publishing Services.

# CONTENTS

REMEMBERING AMERICA

# Introduction

This book is, as the title suggests, a cultural history of American history. More so than intellectual, social, or public histories, which have their own respective agendas, cultural history focuses on the ways in which a particular subject has found expression across a wide swath of everyday life. Surprisingly, no cultural history of American history currently exists, making this admittedly ambitious project an important one. There are innumerable books about some aspect of the history of the United States and no shortage of historiographies of and textbooks on the subject, of course, but no one has yet attempted to tell the fascinating history of American history itself as it was expressed in popular culture and in education.[1]

The irony that the history of American history has been underserved has not been lost. Scholars of all disciplines tend to focus on their area of specialization, often giving little thought to the role of their field within the culture as a whole. American historians past and present have in general overlooked how ripe for study their own subject is, failing to locate it within a broad, contemporary context. A cultural history of American history directly addresses this void by presenting a narrative of the field from both scholarly and popular points of view. With history all around us, a ubiquitous presence in everything, from food to travel to architecture and design, it makes sense that someone takes the time to document its own, compelling story. With this book readers will hopefully gain a much better sense of the important role that the nation's history has played within American Life.

One does not have to be an expert in the field to know that American history has recently become a passionate and divisive political and cultural issue: a broad public debate about the teaching of U.S. history was set off by the very controversial changes made to Texas textbook standards in 2009–10, standards that have wide effect given the large number of textbooks purchased by Texas public schools. The dispute goes to the very heart of how we want to think about and construct our nation's past, and clearly illustrates that American history is very much a living, organic thing rather than simply "what happened." By dramatizing public struggles over what history meant and how to remember it, we get a true sense of how vibrant the subject has been and continues to be.

*Remembering America* makes it vividly clear that the subject deserves its own cultural history. For the past century, American history has been an emotionally charged site that has regularly overlapped into the political and legal arenas. The heart of the story revolves around the principal place U.S. history has occupied within education and, to a lesser extent, popular culture. American history has continually shaped and reflected our cultural values and national identity: how we interpret and express our country's past reveals key insights relating to who we were as a people at different times. The story of American history is thus not a straight line but instead one filled with twists and turns, and ups and downs, its narrative arc as winding as that of the United States as a whole.

More than anything else, however, this book illustrates that American history has played a much more important role in the discourse of everyday life than is commonly recognized. As a famously forward-thinking people far more interested in what is coming around the corner versus what has already passed, Americans have assigned to their own history far less credit than it deserves. American history is, I believe, the Rodney Dangerfield of the humanities (and social sciences, for that matter), getting little or no respect from either academics in other fields or among ordinary folk. (American history's cousin, American studies, has fared somewhat better, but it, too, is generally viewed by the public as an idiosyncratic subject with little real value to offer regarding contemporary affairs.) Since the end of World War I, American history has functioned as a powerful force informing the national conversation in many disparate ways (particularly as a contentious site that has divided as much as united us). We may deny or repress it, but a strong sense of our shared heritage, critically interpreted or otherwise, is in our DNA, making our collective history one of the very few things Americans have in common.

As any history should, this book poses key questions to shed new light on the subject. Were Americans receptive or resistant to historical tellings of their country? What purposes did American history play within the larger cultural climate—that is, what causes were being served? Was history being used to challenge or affirm social values in place at the time? How did history serve the dominant national narrative and how did it critique it (sometimes at the same time)? Answers to such questions help us better understand the cultural history of the United States in different eras. History is, after all, one of our most powerful resources, with the present largely determined by how we remember the past. Fluid and volatile rather than fixed and stable, American history is an ideal barometer for measuring national mood and direction. As editors Edward T. Linenthal and Tom Englehardt showed in their 1996 *History Wars: The Enola Gay and Other Battles for the American Past*, American history often acted as a key site of struggle and contention as different ideological groups fought over "ownership" of the nation's past.[2] Politically charged by both the Left and the Right, the interpretive narrative of American history was essentially up for grabs at any given time, with the "winners" likely to tell stories that supported their particular agenda. American history also operated as a primary means by which we told foreigners who we were (and were not), acting as a kind of diplomat (or propaganda device) that served national and geopolitical interests.

A long view of American history also helps to chart the evolution of society on a number of important levels. The tools we used to tell history changed over the years, of course, with each generation adopting a different form of technology (print, film, radio, television, and the Internet) as its medium of choice. The lines between "fact" and "fiction" were by no means clear, with each era having a different tolerance for "dramatization" and its own mandate for separating mythology from reality. A major theme is the gradual awareness that history was inherently selective (or downright biased), with the "truth" a matter of interpretation (or dispute).

Some argued that truth was less important than the purposes history could and should serve, however, with the teaching of myths a vital part of building character and a patriotic spirit. After World War I, a more scientific, empirically based history emerged that was more truthful in the sense of being less mythical. Over time it became clear that the search for an absolute truth was an elusive one, however; any particular construction of the past was inherently based on interpretation. As American history consistently became multiculturalized over the decades, it became obvious that the nation's official past was heavily skewed toward the interests of privileged white males. The historical voice of people of color, women, and the poor became increasingly louder over the years, causing the present study to necessarily examine the dynamics of race, gender, and class. The attempt to construct a "usable past" represents another consistent theme, with the growing realization that history should ideally serve a function rather than lie dormant and purposeless. Likewise, the shift from American history being seen as a record of events and dates (especially wars and presidential terms) to organic stories of ordinary people's lives becomes another clear and revealing insight.

Finally, the work examines the intersection between American history and young people in considerable detail. For students of all levels, American history was perceived by educators and those outside the field as somehow special, accounting for the passionate feelings that were typically attached to the teaching of the subject. Unlike science or math, say, American history was a subject that was not just academic but directly connected to identity on both the national and individual levels. Survey after survey revealed students' historical illiteracy, with figures of authority routinely alarmed at the lack of knowledge of American history among young people. This deficiency was seen as a direct threat to good citizenship and thus social stability, the notion of a history-less generation devoid of a sense of history becoming a very frightening scenario. Not just the young mind but the future of the nation was viewed as hanging in the balance, with the "wrong" ideas about our past capable of seeding political leanings away from our democratic (and consumerist) American way of life. Textbooks and teachers have served as the primary recipients of blame, each faulted for leaving out the "story" in "history." Efforts to make the subject

more interesting and relevant for students through more innovative pedagogical techniques have been routine, but it is safe to say that American
history remains a "problem" within the educational arena. Strangely, though,
the subject has represented a staple of the entertainment world, with the
nation's past being successfully mined in movies, television shows, books,
and interactive experiences. This disconnect is yet another area worth
investigating, begging the question of how a subject can be wildly popular
in one realm but equally unpopular in another.

This book begins immediately after World War I, when American history,
like virtually everything else on the national scene, was swept up in the
forces of modernity. American history came into its own as both an
academic field and a key site of popular culture following that war. The
flourishing of mass culture through the 1920s offered new opportunities to explore the nation's past, and the ascent of "Progressive" history
that decade marked a clear break from the heavily mythology-based field
of the past. Progressive history was an outgrowth of the Progressive
reform movement that flourished around the turn of the twentieth century as a response to political corruption, inequities of capitalism, and
a multitude of social ills. History, too, had the potential to reform and
improve society, its proponents held; change and progress could be realized via a more critical approach to the history of the United States.
    Clear signs of the maturation of American history could be detected
at the turn of the twentieth century. A large wave of interest in the history
of the country struck Americans as we crossed over into a new century,
something typical of any significant anniversary or benchmark of time.
With the country experiencing rapid and, for many, alarming change
(for example, industrialization, immigration, and urbanization), turn-
of-the-century Americans looked back to their past for security and
comfort. The development of the union, creation of statehoods, and evolution of our national identity were all important themes Americans
pondered as they looked forward to the next hundred years. The settlement of the West (or "possession of the continent," as it was sometimes
called) was of particular interest, with the debate over Manifest Destiny
revived. Migration and expansion—specifically, how and why Americans

of the nineteenth century moved across the country—was used as a primary way to tell the story of United States. The expeditions of Meriwether Lewis and William Clark and of other adventurers were romanticized in a reaction to Frederick Jackson Turner's 1893 announcement that the nation's frontier had been "closed." Folk heroes of the past—notably, Davy Crockett—were similarly lauded as the nation constructed historical mythologies as a buffer against encroaching modernity. Great battles like that at the Alamo and at sea reaffirmed Americans' faith that they were a strong people and could withstand future threats, whatever they may be.

If American history during the first decade of the twentieth century was mostly about looking in the rearview mirror for social ballast, that of the next decade was generally concerned with establishing a clear definition of national identity. A new kind of patriotic fervor swept through the country in the years 1911–19, turning American history into an instrument of nationalism. Our proud past had made us who we were, figures of authority made clear, and served as a lesson to explain the American idea to foreigners. The country's involvement in the Great War made the "Americanization" and "100 percent Americanism" movements that much more urgent, inscribing history with a strong sense of national purpose. At least some of the millions of new immigrants arrived on our shores with "un-American" cultural practices and/or political views, it was feared, necessitating assimilation into the nation's melting pot.

The "Americanization" movement, led by the Woodrow Wilson administration's Committee on Public Information, or Creel Committee, was a massive effort preceding and during the war to instill American ways—especially the speaking of English—into the "huddled masses." The "100 percent Americanism" movement was a post–World War I attempt led by President Wilson to celebrate all things American and assail foreignness in all its forms. History thus became seen as a tool of Americanization and Americanism (and ultimately assimilation), a means to crush divisiveness, social unrest, and "radicalism." Immigrants wishing to be U.S. citizens were required to take a course in American history, and this is a good example of how the country's past was appropriated as a vehicle of solidarity and unity in a time of considerable social and cultural upheaval. By 1920 the stage was set for American history to blossom into a much different and bigger dimension of everyday life, which is where I pick up this fascinating story.

*Remembering America* tells its story chronologically, beginning at the end of World War I and going right up to today. The backbone of the book relies on contemporary, popular sources (as a cultural history should), as well as scholarly journals and other books. Hundreds of different sources are used, drawing from journalists' and scholars' writing of "the first draft of history." American history has, of course, served as a key theme in movies, television, books, and leisure activities, and these also serve as prime fodder for this study.

Chapter 1, "The Epic of America," takes readers from the 1920s through the mid-1940s, when American history emerged as a contentious site and the very purpose of the field was questioned. Chapter 2, "E Pluribus Unum," examines American history during the postwar years, when the Cold War was instrumental in raising the profile of the subject in both academia and popular culture. Chapter 3, "E Pluribus Confusion," explores American history in the late 1960s and 1970s, when the counterculture fragmented the field and ushered in new kinds of critical interpretations of the country's past. Assimilation, since the early part of the century, became discredited in favor of multiculturalism, as Gary Gerstle showed in his book *American Crucible*, part of a major shift in national identity.[3] As a backlash, perhaps, conservatism, a minority viewpoint during the New Deal era, experienced a rebirth starting in the 1970s; beginning in that decade conservatives operated from a much stronger position and articulated a more full-throated critique of the culture, history included, through the last quarter of the twentieth century.

Chapter 4, "The Fall of the American Adam," shows how the field became increasingly polarized and politicized, so much so that some wondered if a core component of American history still existed. Chapter 5, "We the Peoples," investigates American history in the 1990s, when the "culture wars" further intensified the tensions in the field. Chapter 6, "The Fray of History," tells the story of American history in the early twenty-first century, when a concerted, massive effort was made to try to reinvigorate the field. The future of American history remains unclear, I note in the conclusion of this book, as the gap between the field's status in education and popular culture continues to widen. Bridging this gap is essential to making American history a subject that is attractive to young people, something that I believe is entirely possible.

# 1 The Epic of America

1920–1945

> It is well that we should take pride in our national past; but it is certainly not to be desired that we should view that past through some haze of false sentiment, or twist the facts for the purpose of patriotic propaganda.
>
> Dexter Perkins, "America Rewrites Her History"

In 1923 a statute was passed by the Wisconsin legislature that regulated the ways in which American history was taught in that state's public schools. No textbook, the act read, could be used in classes "which falsifies the facts regarding the war of independence, or the war of 1812, or which defames our nation's founders or misrepresents the ideals and causes for which they struggled and sacrificed, or which contains propaganda favorable to any foreign government." All school boards in the state had to discontinue the use of any textbook that violated the law or else lose their public funding.[1]

A state enacting a law about school textbooks was (and thankfully is) unusual, to say the least. Even at the time, some historians were fully aware of the peculiarity of the new Wisconsin statute. Soon after the act was passed, an editor for the *American Historical Review* wrote that it "merits exhibition in the pages of an historical journal, not only on account of the grave considerations which it raises in connection with present-day teaching, but also as a curiosity, to be preserved for readers in future years, who may examine it with the same interest with which, in museums of domestic antiquities, we look at old tin lanterns and candle-moulds, wondering at the quaint inadequate means of illumination with which our predecessors contented themselves."[2]

While certainly extreme, Wisconsin's concern over American history textbooks was representative of the turmoil in the field between the world wars. Many were not prepared for the writing and teaching of histories that did not somehow favor the United States, an outgrowth of the pursuit for objective and scientific facts that so defined the times. Truth increasingly clashed with myth in American history in the 1920s and 1930s, a contentious process that would ultimately and permanently redefine the field. "Progressive" historians with a more critical view of the nation's past challenged those of the previous generation, raising serious questions about the very purpose of studying American history. An idea that historians of all ideological leanings could agree on was that the American story was a rich and powerful one that could function as a resource to help guide the country through whatever cataclysmic events might lie ahead. Indeed, America's story was epic in scope and, as James Truslow Adams, the most popular historian of the times, expressed it, a foundation that would pave the way for an even greater future. In order to achieve this grand mission, however, Americans had to possess a thorough knowledge of their nation's history, something that appeared to be highly questionable.

### A Steady, Persistent Endeavor

Just as World War I marked a major turning point in many spheres of life in the United States, the "war to end all wars" deeply affected the American school system. Specifically, the war catalyzed scholars to reexamine how textbooks presented the nation's involvement in previous wars. The "Americanization" programs during the Great War no doubt had something to do with historians' urge to rewrite the nation's wartime past in a more critical fashion. In part as a reaction or backlash to the unchecked jingoism that was pushed on the American public by the United States Committee on Public Information, headed by George Creel during the administration of President Woodrow Wilson, some academics embarked on a mission to expose the less savory aspects of American history, especially in regard to foreign relations. Historians published new interpretations of the Revolutionary War, the War of 1812, and the Monroe Doctrine soon after World War I that painted a picture of the country and its political leaders as considerably less glorious than standard American history textbooks depicted. In place since the mid-nineteenth century, the heavily mythic version of American history was fading as more truthful revelations about the nation's past emerged.[3]

Members of more conservative and traditional organizations were not happy to see American history turned into something quite different from what it had been. In 1921, for example, the Knights of Columbus, the Catholic fraternal benefit society, launched an initiative to counteract this new wave of history that was beginning to take hold in the nation's schools. Describing themselves simply as "pro-American," the Knights offered thousands of dollars in cash to professors of history, school superintendents and teachers, and students who subscribed to and promoted their movement. The organization estimated it would spend a whopping $1 million to write, produce, and distribute thousands of pamphlets and scores of monographs, all of this output designed to stem the rising tide of "anti-American" sentiment in American history schoolbooks. The millions of immigrants arriving on America's shores comprised a special audience the Knights of Columbus wanted to reach with their campaign, clearly fearing that critical interpretations of American history could help breed a powerful subversive element that threatened our democracy. The organization was committed to putting into place "a steady, persistent endeavor to aid in supplying [a] background of correct and complete knowledge of the national genesis and evolution without which citizenship must ever remain spiritually imperfect," declared John B. Kennedy, the chairman of the Knights' history commission.[4]

Other patriotic organizations acted to try to stop what they viewed as a menacing intruder in its tracks. As could be expected, members of the Sons of the American Revolution were very perturbed to see young, relatively unknown historians turn the tables on the most defining moment in the country's history. Censoring textbooks that misrepresented the founding of the nation and its chief architects was perfectly appropriate, the society made clear—an ironic stance given the freedoms the group held in such high regard. W. I. Lincoln Adams, the aptly named president of the Sons of the American Revolution, detailed his organization's position in *Current History* in 1922. "It is astonishing to find how many of those who are attempting to teach American history are not in sympathy with their subject," he wrote, believing that those who entered the field should by default have a nationalistic ideological view. Socialists, communists, and agnostics were determined to destroy "the acts and motives of our heroes and the great leaders of our past," Adams continued, the authors of recently published textbooks as much at fault as misguided teachers. Hero worship was good for young people, he and many others argued, convinced that adolescent boys' "manhood" would suffer if idols such as George Washington, Alexander Hamilton, and Abraham Lincoln were depicted as ordinary, flawed people.[5]

Actual adolescent boys, meanwhile, were less interested in developing their "manhood" than in reading books about American history that were challenging and provocative, according to Julia Houston Railey. Clever young people were in fact tired of the mythic kind of American history that filled books for juveniles at the time, she wrote in *Outlook* in 1923, with little change in the publishing genre since the mid-nineteenth century. Too many stories involved savage Indians or the moralistic deeds of George Washington, youthful but experienced readers felt, the standard literary clichés making them yearn for books with more substance and truth. (Benjamin Franklin's kite experiment was another classic repeated ad nauseam.) It could be argued that children's books consisted of an unusual number of courageous, self-sacrificing Puritans and pioneers, their portrayal recognized by smarter boys and girls as overly simplistic and ungenuine. Revolutionary war generals also frequently appeared in both fiction and nonfiction, their leadership skills clearly intended as an instructive device and their heroism designed to instill a patriotic spirit. Some great reading certainly lay ahead—James Fenimore Cooper's and Mark Twain's novels, notably—but, until their teenage years, brainier children interested in American history had little to choose from library bookshelves and in the classroom.[6]

### The Fundamental Test of History

Books directed to an adult—and, specifically, academic—audience, however, posed the bigger problem in American history. As Progressive historians challenged accepted but unproven (and often highly suspicious) suppositions about the nation's past in the 1920s, the entire field suffered a kind of mass identity crisis. Those invested in the field asked themselves what the purpose of writing and teaching American history was, but the answer to that fundamental question was not at all clear. Was it to build a stronger citizenship, or to tell, as Walter Hart Blumenthal expressed it in 1927, "the unvarnished truth"? Blumenthal, an encyclopedia editor, firmly believed it was the latter, taking issue with the position of many educators who argued that the field held an important social responsibility to promote patriotism and "wholesomeness" among children. Any kind of criticism directed at the "great men" of the nation's past was popularly viewed as wrong and, in some cases, a kind of disloyal threat. In fact, in many public schools at the time (including not just those in Wisconsin but also those in New York City), no textbook that was "derogatory" or "disparaged the achievements of American heroes" was allowed to be used, nor one that "questioned the sincerity of the aims and purposes of the founders of the Republic." A strict, narrow interpretation of the key events and players of American history was best for children, agreed most educators in the late 1920s, with no icon to be toppled, no legend to be destroyed, no flag to be desecrated. "The holy ghost of patriotism must not be besmirched," Blumenthal noted, with no challenges to our nationalist faith officially tolerated.[7]

Such a position was becoming increasingly difficult to maintain, however, as a new group of historians changed the status quo. Many if not most scholars who received their academic training after World War I had a different point of view about the American experience than did those who got their degrees before it. The horrors of that war and the widespread feelings of alienation and cynicism following it among young adults famously shaped an entire generation, including those committed to studying the nation's past. Equally if not more important was the rise of science after the war, with historians prone to embrace a more systematic approach in their own field. Recording facts drawn from official documents was increasingly seen as the historical equivalent to scientific analysis, a method that was considered superior to the folklore of the past. In this new kind of cultural climate, the mythologies of the old order were now vulnerable to being torn down and replaced by a more truthful representation of what had taken place. Not just historians in the United States but those in Europe were interested in what they saw as a distorted account of the American past. Discussions about "tradition versus fact" became a central issue at history conferences in England, with the portrayal of the British during the Revolutionary War a particular sore spot among scholars and political leaders across the pond. Although a century and a half had passed, many Brits objected to the way in which American history textbooks cast their forefathers as villains. There was another side to the story, they insisted, as evidenced by a growing number of books whose aim was to correct the record and offer a more balanced perspective of that conflict.[8]

One did not need a PhD from an Ivy League college to find bits of American history that traditionalists would consider objectionable or embarrassing to our nation's legacy. For one thing, colonists in New England were actually a lot less pious than was commonly believed, with the widespread knowledge of such perhaps seen by some as a threat to the country's Judeo-Christian ethic. Drinking, on the other hand, was one of Yankees' favorite pastimes. As well, profiteering—charging excessively high prices for scarce goods—was business as usual for the entrepreneurial in the late eighteenth century. Most potentially damning was the fact that new Americans were hardly as fond of the Founding Fathers and the government they had created as subsequent generations would be; they saw any kind of federal entity as virtually as foreign and oppressive as the British. Politicians were far more corrupt and autocratic than we like to remember, and our most treasured asset—freedom of speech—was sometimes difficult to locate. And as those who took the time and made the effort would learn, a good chunk of nineteenth-century history was as fictional as that of the eighteenth. The veracity of the outcome of certain Civil War battles was questionable, for example, and it could not be disputed that Abraham Lincoln came within a whisker of not even getting on the ballot for the 1860 presidential election. The "good old days" were not as good as they generally seemed, it could safely be said, and this was something that a growing number of historians believed more Americans should know.[9]

David Saville Muzzey, a professor at Barnard College and one of the foremost authors of American history textbooks, was one of about ten top scholars determined to permanently retire yesterday's way of looking at the nation's past. Muzzey argued that American history was still largely stuck in how the subject was taught in the 1870s and 1880s, just a few decades after the field came into being. He noted that the first generation of textbooks was built mainly on Revolutionary War legends and designed to compete with the dime novels so popular with boys of the time, making these transcribed oral histories wholly unreliable. As well, melodrama was the dominant form of entertainment in the late nineteenth century, a factor that contributed heavily to the stereotyped characters, exaggerated emotions, simplistic morality, and over-the-top conflict that filled the books. Oratory, the art of speaking in public, also played a major social and political role in the Victorian era; this, too, contributed to the dramatic, almost theatrical style of American history textbooks. Attempts to separate the wheat from the chaff, metaphorically speaking, were considered suspect. Oddly enough, scholarly research was viewed as a meddlesome pursuit at the time, the danger being, of course, that the popular legends would be exposed as just that. That had all changed by the late 1920s, however, as the immense influence of the scientific method spread into not just the social sciences but the humanities.[10]

Arguments from both sides of the fence filled American history journals in the 1920s, with most academics pleading a case for truth no matter what the social cost. "Truth is the fundamental test of history and there is no such thing as American truth," wrote Lyon G. Tyler, editor of *Tyler's Quarterly Historical Magazine*, in 1928, trying to put to rest the row between traditionalists and the group of authors of American history textbooks who had put "truth" ahead of patriotism. For Tyler, a historian had just two responsibilities: to use facts and to make deductions from these facts in an impartial manner. There was enough heroism in the nation's past without a historian having to embellish the facts, he believed, and there was plenty of patriotism to be found in textbooks if that was what one wanted to glean from them.[11]

Not everyone, however, believed young people should be told the whole truth about the American past. Because adolescents were not yet mature and not trained to think analytically, some argued, it could be harmful to disclose to them the less attractive aspects about a particular hero's character. "There are certain facts concerning the private acts of some of the 'Fathers of the Republic' that are not to their credit, but would be, I think, a detriment in helping to form an estimate of the man as one should be judged by his public deeds," wrote Mary E. McDowell, founder of the University of Chicago Settlement House (a kindergarten and nursery school). The revelation that a great man liked to drink (General Ulysses S. Grant, notably) or gamble (Henry Clay, it was said) might detract from an appreciation for what he did for the country, McDowell felt, and hers was a legitimate point. Private life was separate from public life, in other words—a distinction that would repeatedly be raised when some unsavory revelation was made about an elected official or when he was at the center of some sort of scandal.[12]

Dana Carleton Munro, former president of the American Historical Association and professor of history at Princeton University, on the other hand, argued in 1928 that truthful history could build character just as well as if not better than any fabricated version. It would be silly for any adult to think that any individual, living or dead, was completely faultless, or that the country as a whole had never done anything wrong. Teaching "perfecthood" to children would thus be wrong, he pointed out, by making them believe in a flawless person or society when neither could truly exist. Learning the more negative aspect of American history could actually be as constructive as learning the more positive facets, he added—a lesson to be gained by an awareness of the mistakes and misdeeds of the past if presented in the correct way. Young people were smarter than many adults credited them to be, able to see through lies and detect shams orchestrated by parents and teachers for youths' supposed benefit.[13]

### The Firmament of Patriotism

As the quest for truth became increasingly paramount in the field, many of the myths central to teaching American history to young people were breaking down by the late 1920s. Military history, especially, was vulnerable to the debunking of the legends and fables that had over the years become accepted as truth. Interestingly enough, many military men themselves preferred the truth when it was known over the popular stories, feeling that the efforts of the nation's armed forces over the last century and a half needed no embellishment. "American military history has most commonly been expounded by sentimental patriots to the accompaniment of wildly waving flags and an utter disregard of facts or political implications," wrote Elbridge Colby in 1928, thinking it was his duty to correct the record. Colby, a captain in the U.S. Army, cited a litany of examples that portrayed our military as significantly less heroic than popularly believed. From the Revolutionary War through World War I, he explained, our army was often unprepared, undertrained, and overfunded, a much different story from that usually told in schoolbooks (and by politicians).[14]

Colby's depiction of the country's military history was indeed a lot less pretty than the virtually unblemished one taught in schools and recounted in speeches. George Washington's withdrawal from New York City in 1776 was more of a messy retreat than the brilliant tactical move it had somehow become in the popular imagination; the Battle of Long Island that same year was less a marginal defeat for the Americans than a complete trouncing brought on by the British; and the capture of the city of Washington in the War of 1812 was not at all the overpowering victory it was commonly documented to have been. Similar tall tales had been told about battles in the Civil War, the Spanish-American War of 1898, and World War I, Colby added, with the reality obscured in the name of patriotism and glory. Colby subscribed to the ideas of Colonel Oliver L. Spaulding Jr., a former officer at the Army War College, who argued that the beautification of our military history was doing more damage than good. War was a part of political life, meaning that children, as future voters, should know the truth about how it had been waged in the past. Not teaching that truth was bordering on criminal behavior, Spaulding proposed, as elected officials would continue to send men into battle based on a set of false beliefs.[15]

Rupert Hughes, author of a biography of George Washington, agreed with Colby that American history could use a generous dose of honesty and frankness. Writing in the same issue of *Current History*, Hughes defended the growing number of historians who were under attack for challenging the myths that pervaded the field. Scholars simply trying to uncover or tell the truth (such as a very young Arthur Schlesinger, author of the controversial *New Viewpoints in American History*) were being called traitors and treasonous by conservatives. Some of the former were even accused of accepting bribes from the British to write or teach histories of the Revolutionary War that somehow portrayed America in an unfavorable light. The minds of Americans, particularly those of children, were being poisoned by this kind of propaganda, claimed Chicago mayor William "Big Bill" Thompson, among others. "Drop the heroes from the country's histories," Thompson wrote, "and you take the stars out of the firmament of patriotism."[16] Labeled "treasonous" by Thompson, authors of textbooks defended their right (and responsibility) to tell the truth about the nation's idols even if it involved shattering the prevailing myths surrounding them.[17] Muzzey, in fact, was suing a Chicago elected official for $100,000 for making such an allegation, knowing that history was on his side. The libel suit was dismissed, however, when the official, John C. Gorman, issued a formal statement declaring that he had never even read the textbooks Muzzey found so propagandist.[18]

Thompson and his compatriots were especially irked about the recent trend in American history to label George Washington as a rebel and traitor (against England), a view that the mayor believed tarnished the great man's reputation. (As an authority on the matter, Hughes pointed out that Washington "was nothing at all" if not a rebel and traitor to his king and country, a fact that enhanced rather than diminished the man's image.) Other objectionable statements made by this new breed of historians were that John Hancock was a "smuggler," Samuel Adams was "the first American political boss," and Patrick Henry was "an unprosperous and unknown country lawyer"; these, too, were considered by some to be defamatory in nature. Alexander Hamilton's remark, "The people, sir, is a great beast," was better left unrepeated, as were certain observations made by Thomas Jefferson, James Madison, and other Founding Fathers that were less than diplomatic. Loving one's country and being critical of it were simply incompatible to "patriots" like Thompson who urged that the facts be suppressed if they were known. "Are we to define patriotism as an emotion based solely on fables and ignorance?" Hughes sensibly asked.[19]

## A Better, Deeper, Richer Life

Like World War I, the stock market crash of 1929 and subsequent Great Depression would alter the trajectory of American history. Worries over "the unvarnished truth" were, for the most part, put aside in the 1930s as the field of American history was assigned the greater purpose of raising morale during the devastating economic crisis. American folklife of the past was celebrated during the Depression, the distinction between reality and mythology being deemed less important than affirmations of the country's greatness. Yesterday's pioneers and farmers in particular achieved legendary status in books, art, theater, and films of the decade, a prime instance of how history can serve as a "usable past." In its treatment of the Civil War and Reconstruction, *Gone with the Wind*, both the novel and film, affirmed traditional values of home and family arguably more than any other novel or movie of the 1930s. As a romanticized version of life on a slaveholding plantation, it (like *The Birth of a Nation*) also reinforced racial stereotypes, a regretful act but as powerful a use of American history as can be imagined.

The "American Dream" was another seminal historical trope of the 1930s. That the term was created in the darkest days of the Great Depression was all the more interesting given that many feared that such a dream couldn't exist. In his 1931 book *The Epic of America* and in articles published in the *New York Times* the following few years, best-selling author and historian James Truslow Adams defined what he meant by the American Dream, an idea whose essence has remained largely consistent these past eighty years; in one *New York Times Magazine* article he wrote, "The dream is a vision of a better, deeper, richer life for every individual, regardless of the position in society which he or she may occupy by the accident of birth. It has been a dream of a chance to rise in the economic scale, but quite as much, or more than that, of a chance to develop our capacities to the full, unhampered by unjust restrictions of caste or custom."[20]

Adams argued, however, that in the late 1920s, as in previous periods of overexpansion and out-of-control speculation, the nation had lost its way and its guiding philosophy had been forgotten in the wild pursuit of money and the things it could buy. The market crash and subsequent depression were a natural (and, for Adams, predictable) result of this collective greed, but the dream of "a richer, better, fuller human life for all citizens" could be revived. The nation having survived its "mental disorder," Adams was hopeful that its vision would be restored. "Like the passing of the shadow in an eclipse, the light of reason appears to be steadily extending over the horizon," he believed, and the American Dream was beginning to reemerge.[21]

Adams, modestly describing himself as a "student of history and surveyor of the American scene" (he was the most commercially successful historian of his day), was well aware that his dream was much more than just a noble idea. "That dream is not only our most precious national possession but our only unique contribution to the civilization of the world," he wrote after spending a few months abroad in 1933, noting that many other societies past and present matched or surpassed the United States in wealth, power, discoveries, inventions, science, crafts, and the arts. But "the American dream has been unique in the social annals of mankind," he observed, its "dynamic belief" the thing that separated it from the rest of the pack. More so than other fundamental ideals—equality before the law and every citizen's right to vote and to an education, notably—it was Americans' "opportunity of rising to full stature and living the fullest possible life" that was truly special. Importantly, the American Dream in its original incarnation was thus not about getting rich, owning a piece of property, working for oneself, or some other later interpretation but, in Adams's words, the "inherent right to be restricted by no barriers" outside those of one's own construction. That the dream was intangible made it all the more intriguing to Adams, despite the inescapable fact that it had yet to be fully realized (especially among women and people of color, most obviously).[22]

Adams's best-selling book, with its thesis that we are and always have been a nation of dreamers, quickly captured people's attention. The book sold 358,000 copies in 1931—a terrible year in the Depression—and was translated into eight foreign languages, each a clear indication that the general public found it compelling reading. (It was widely considered the best single-volume history of the United States available at the time.) Reviewers immediately recognized that Adams had produced a very important work. H. S. Commager of *Books* considered it "a courageous attempt to put the quintessence of American experience and character into brief compass," and Karl Schriftglesser of the *Boston Transcript* called it "a keen analysis of the American mind."[23] While some critics thought Adams had perhaps overreached in his ambitious thesis, most felt he had deftly translated some very complex concepts into simple and understandable terms. "In a mass of current historical writing, much of which is ephemeral or discursive, here is a book vibrant with ideas that have a meaning for every reflective American," wrote Allen Sinclair Will in his review for the *New York Times*, thinking Adams's "audacious attempt" of capturing the epic of America had matched or perhaps even bettered that of Walt Whitman. Rather than defining the epic as a heroic tale of a people with superior spirit and morality—a standard approach of many historians up to that point—Adams suggested that Americans had often taken the path of least resistance when times got tough. It was quite an assertion. Our greatest achievement was not that we were a shining beacon for all the world to see but that each generation had saved the American Dream from forces that threatened to destroy it; this, he felt, was the true epic of the nation. "Possibly the greatest of these struggles lies just ahead of us," Adams proposed in the book, and it was a prophecy that would turn out to be true.[24]

Though not the title of his book as Adams wanted it (the publisher nixed his idea to name it *The American Dream*), the term was soon appropriated by politicians, scholars, writers, artists, religious leaders, and many others, both in the United States and abroad, to describe the nation's state of affairs. The American Dream "entered the public domain . . . and took on a life of its own," Anthony Brandt reflected on the fiftieth anniversary of the publishing of *The Epic of America*, noting that governor Joseph B. Ely of Massachusetts was quick to use it in a speech made in front of the monument on Bunker Hill. Ely tweaked the meaning of the phrase to match the particular occasion, something that would to this day become more the rule than the exception. (Adams himself provided at least three slightly different definitions of the American Dream in his book, and would continue to modify the term in his future writings.) As soon as the book's ink was dry, "the boundaries of the phrase was becoming increasingly vague, a development to be expected from the vagueness implicit in the very notion of a 'dream,' of a dimly perceived vision of possible futures," Brandt suggested. In an essay published a few years later, for example, sociologist Robert K. Merton took the phrase to mean success, especially in the financial sense, further arguing that this was Americans' primary goal. But Merton himself recognized the infinite possibilities of the American Dream ("there is no final stopping point," he wrote), with this being perhaps its most salient aspect. "The Dream stretches endlessly and forever toward the horizon," Brandt agreed, "the lure of 'more' and 'better' pulling us on, no matter what we accomplish, individually or collectively."[25]

## The Pageant of American Life

A couple of years after Adams's landmark book was published, Herbert E. Bolton made the case that while *The Epic of America* was undoubtedly brilliant, it had one serious liability: it essentially ignored the role of the United States from an international perspective. "The epic of greater America," as he called it, would locate the history of the country in a broader context, something he felt was necessary in the increasingly global political climate of the 1930s. Writing in the *American Historical Review*, Bolton, a professor at the University of California–Berkeley, argued that American history was currently overly nationalistic and that a "synthetic" view would go a long way toward remedying our myopic interpretation of the past. We had a lot more in common with other Americas than we liked to believe, he stated, with many countries sharing a similar colonial experience. "A noted historian has written for us *The Epic of America*, Bolton concluded, pressing the need for "an Adams to sketch the high lights and the significant developments of the Western Hemisphere as a whole."[26]

A comparative approach to studying American history could indeed reveal key, largely overlooked insights. U.S. history was significantly shorter than other "modern" nations, for example, but it did have a few outstanding characteristics. First, unlike that of many European or Asian countries, American history was "coherent," meaning it could be viewed and understood as a whole (in part because of its relative brevity); second, it was especially well documented, as the colonists were almost obsessive about writing memoirs and reproducing important papers; and third, it held unusually powerful symbolic value. European history was gradual and complicated, it could be said, while American history was swift and relatively simple—at least so it was believed at the time. Although brief, the nation's past was jam-packed with material that would make a novelist proud, with this no doubt contributing to the fact that history was by far a bigger and more lucrative business here than anywhere else. (Biographies had long been popular in the United States, while Europeans had only recently become keen on reading a book about a noteworthy person's life.) Americans were as a rule consumer-minded and social, but it was history that united the people, one might argue, and this explained why it held such a special place in the national consciousness.[27]

The field's scholarly evolution was a more complicated affair. As an academic discipline, American history had taken a major turn in the late 1870s and early 1880s, when universities borrowed heavily upon the methods of German scholarship. Investigations into more defined areas, such as the Germans were known for, became accepted practice in the field, an approach that allowed for more precision and closer study of a particular topic. Works about the temperance movement, the "peace crusade," and the public health movement had been published in the late nineteenth century, for example, creating a new kind of American history that would become standard in the field. Another significant shift in the field took place after World War I, when scholars ventured into social and intellectual histories as an alternative or complement to the customary political and economic histories of the day. With their respective social points of view, works that came between the wars—such as *The Pageant of American Life* and *A History of American Life*—were unlike anything published before, foreshadowing the interdisciplinary approach to history that would soon lead to the creation of the field of American studies. Finally, themes that represented significant dimensions of the American experience (that is, religion and the West) had become subfields all their own, this too being a sign of bigger things to come.[28]

As the United States began to crawl out of the Depression in the mid-1930s, historians again had the luxury to disagree with each other over what was best for the field. Some historians, notably Theodore Clarke Smith of Williams College, believed the field had essentially split in two by that time. One group shared, in Smith's words, "a noble dream," that dream being the search for the "objective truth" of the past. The other group consisted of those who relied heavily upon an economic interpretation of American history, this for Smith being a violation of the former's all-encompassing pursuit of truth. Speaking for the latter, unnamed group (clearly the Progressives), Charles A. Beard, the most influential academic historian of the first half of the twentieth century, defended the use of economics as a lens through which to view the nation's past. "The historian who searches out and orders economic aspects of life, events, and interests may possibly be as zealous in his search for truth as any other historian searching out and ordering his facts in his way," he wrote in the *American Historical Review* in 1935, denying that all Progressives owed a heavy debt to the theories of Karl Marx. Beard also made it clear that Progressives were not necessarily partisan or doctrinaire, as Smith claimed; Beard insisted that his group was simply interested in addressing "the wider and deeper philosophical questions" of American history.[29]

Not choosing sides in the ideological battle was perhaps the biggest cheerleader for American history in the 1930s—Franklin Delano Roosevelt. "The older I grow and the more I read history," the president told a Little Rock, Arkansas, audience on his 1936 campaign tour, "the more I reflect upon the influence of men and events of one generation upon the life and thought of the generations that follow." FDR had actually already announced that the theme of that campaign would be historical in nature in an attempt to link the past to his New Deal. By doing so, he cleverly reckoned, the domestic economic programs he had put into place over the course of his first term would appear less radical, as the Republicans charged. For the next few months Roosevelt referenced in his speeches such historical instances as the Louisiana Purchase, Texas farmers' rebellion against the railroads' monopoly, and George Rogers Clark's battle for conservation in Indiana, all of them somehow relating to New Deal expenditures.[30]

FDR found American history to be a useful tool, and continued to use it to further his political agenda in his next term. In a 1939 address to Congress, for example, the president cited Jefferson's shipping embargo of 1807–9 and the burning of the Capitol in 1814 in his appeal to amend the Neutrality Acts. (Roosevelt wanted to send military aid to countries in Europe after the Nazis invaded Poland, something not then possible because of those laws passed during a period of strong isolationist sentiment.) Although FDR took a loose interpretation of the facts surrounding those events in order to set a precedent, his apparent mastery of American history did seem impressive, something that perhaps contributed to his legacy as a great president.[31]

Americans, of course, had things other than history to ponder in the 1930s. The Great Depression was economically and socially devastating for many, if not most, and the Dust Bowl inflicted immense ecological and agricultural damage. Also weighing heavily on the minds of many Americans in the 1930s was the escalating war in Europe. It is important to remember that before the bombings at Pearl Harbor, Americans were hardly united on the subject of whether the country should enter the war. As the debate over isolation versus involvement escalated in 1941, James Truslow Adams took the time to put the clash into historical perspective. "In the past, in times of crisis, the nation has always united," he wrote in the *New York Times Magazine* five months before America entered the war, confident that the country would soon come together on the heated issue. Given the country's extreme diversity, especially along the lines of race and religion, it was remarkable that the people of the United States would find common ground when it was necessary. Conflict prevailed before all the major wars, Adams reminded readers, making the current divisive climate more the rule than the exception. Unity ultimately triumphed, however, with the colonies banding together despite major differences in order to fight the British, the North and South building a stronger nation after their bitter battle, and Americans from many ethnic backgrounds and ideological positions enlisting in the cause to win the Great War. Our commitment to nationhood and our freedoms (for white males, anyway) trumped everything else, Adams—clearly not a Progressive—argued, his optimistic prediction turning out to be 100 percent correct.[32]

## A Proud Comradeship

As would be expected, another world war reoriented the geography of American history. Much of wartime American history was, of course, an exercise in patriotism, and specifically an opportunity to retrace the building of democracy. Wartime films such as *Yankee Doodle Dandy* and *Meet Me in St. Louis* looked back to an America of earlier, more innocent times, offering audiences ballast in the cultural turbulence. In schools, teachers mined legendary stories of the nation's past for use in pageants, plays, and songs, with the federal government happy to provide material that grounded the war in the nation's democratic ideals. Those on the home front were encouraged to visit historically significant places, especially battle sites like Gettysburg, or to retrace the steps of the Founding Fathers. Kids made dioramas of famous events in American history, and took class trips to local historical sites as lessons in the nation's endurance. The history of the presidency was a hot topic, with some suggesting that FDR had served one term too many and others wondering how Jefferson might have managed the war. Our alleged close partnership with England over the past century and a half was touted (though it was actually not all that close until World War II), with little mention of our less than amicable relationship with that country in past centuries. Some historians were particularly interested in the history of propaganda in this country, and specifically the ways in which the government had rallied support for World War I.

World War II served as additional evidence that disruptive events— especially wars—were "good" for American history by triggering the need or desire to perceive the nation within the framework of an extended period of time. Unquestionably, looking back (and forward) has been helpful in locating the country and its place in the world beyond the current crisis, functioning as an agent of stability and balance. Such was the case during World War II, an event that brought attention to both the nation's past and future. With expectations for loyalty and unity, the war, much like World War I, stirred up interest in the country's history. A broad and thorough awareness of our collective past made us a stronger force, many believed, making American history an invisible yet powerful weapon in winning the war. The U.S. Army was even teaching American history to soldiers at basic training camps, thinking that a stronger understanding of the nation's past would compel the men to fight harder to defend their country. The military brass believed that knowing how Americans acted bravely in previous wars would be especially useful, capable of instilling greater patriotism, heroism, and comradeship among the men.[33]

Not surprisingly, then, American history was closely scrutinized during the war years, and specifically as to how young people were being educated in the subject. "No nation can be patriotic in the best sense, so people can feel a proud comradeship, without a knowledge of the past," wrote Allan Nevins, professor of American history at Columbia University, thinking the subject could be a valuable resource both on the home front and front lines. Many agreed that the nation's youth were not as well versed in American history as they could and should be. Students may have been familiar with the great figures of American history, but not as familiar with less famous men and women, and a solid knowledge of the chronology of important events or order of presidents was believed to be lacking. (Knowing whether James Polk came before Franklin Pierce or if it was the other way around, for instance, was viewed as more than trivial when history was largely perceived as a collection of facts.) Causality was also considered deficient, with students perhaps aware of most major events but not the relationships among them. "The fact is that our educational requirements in American history and government have been and are deplorably haphazard, chaotic and ineffective," Nevins grumbled in a belief that nothing less than a major overhaul of the subject was needed.[34]

Those of a certain age could remember the resurgence of American history during the previous world war as part of the large (and oppressive) effort to "Americanize" the country's diverse population. During World War I, many states had passed laws requiring public schools to fulfill certain requirements and follow minimum standards in the teaching of the subject. After the war, however, these laws were repealed, weakened, or ignored, allowing the subject to slide into an acute state of unevenness on a national level. By the early 1940s the requirements and standards regarding the teaching of American history in public schools varied widely from state to state, if they existed at all. The most common requirement (in forty of forty-eight states) was that students had to be taught in some way about the U.S. Constitution; almost half of the states, however, required no general course in American history at all. How long a general course had to be was also inconsistent, with some states mandating a year and others not specifying any length of time.[35]

Other problems plagued the study of the past as the nation did everything it could to ensure that it would have a future. How—or *if*—American history was taught differed greatly not just state by state but also city by city. Chicago, for example, required the subject to be taught in all public high schools for two semesters, but other cities in Illinois made no such demand. Some schools were dropping an academic approach to the subject entirely in favor of one that got students involved in the "making" of history, a well-intentioned but dubious effort. (More than a few wigwams and log cabins were being built in classrooms based on the premise that this would be a good way for students to learn what life was like on the frontier in the nineteenth century.) Finally, American history continued to become absorbed into social studies or world history, and this was another major factor in the subject's waning between the world wars. Social studies was (and remains, I believe) too broad a field to accommodate the depth, nuances, and sheer quantity of American history. Educators with a grasp of the history of the subject itself wistfully looked back to the end of the last century, when there seemed to be no confusion about what American history was or how it should be taught. The subject was more popular then among students from elementary school to high school, making the Gilded Age indeed appear to be the golden days of American history.[36]

Things were not much better on the collegiate level during World War II. Very few colleges and universities required students to take a course in American history, in part due to the emphasis on electives in higher education. At some colleges, in fact, freshmen were not even permitted to take American history, a decision based largely on the false assumption that incoming students already had a solid grounding in the subject. (English, a foreign language, and a science, meanwhile, were often mandatory.) On a more fundamental level, history, unlike subjects such as the classics or theology, had not been part of the core curriculum of American colleges as those institutions had developed over the past century or two. History—and even more so a particular specialty in the field, like American history—was simply not a priority for most higher education institutions, making it no surprise that many students were not attracted to the subject. The result was that at many colleges and universities (including Harvard University), more than half of graduates had never taken a single course in American history. As a direct reaction to young people's lack of familiarity with American history during the war, colleges were trying different things to draw students to the field. Harvard was offering a "guided reading" course to allow flexibility, while Princeton had recently rebranded American history as "American heritage." These were, however, cosmetic modifications. Something significantly bigger was needed to solve the history problem in the United States, Nevins and others believed, with no clear answer in sight to what that would be.[37]

Paradoxically, perhaps, a big factor in the slighting of American history was the simple fact that there was more of it than there used to be. The subject had become much more complicated and complex over the years as the country experienced major challenges (notably, immigration, the development of the West, and race relations), something that may have discouraged more people from engaging in the field. Simpler stories, based either in fact or fiction, may have been a more attractive proposition to both students and teachers than the divisive and conflict-based narrative that emerged between the world wars. In addition to the exponential increase in content, the field itself was transformed in the early decades of the twentieth century. In 1900 history was essentially viewed as a record of noteworthy political events and military actions, making the study of it mostly a matter of memorization and interpretation. Between the wars a variety of new and different kinds of history—social, cultural, economic, and diplomatic—had been added to the mix, with this also making the field thornier and more convoluted.[38]

Comparing American history as an academic subject in the 1940s to what it was at the turn of the century or even after World War I was thus not quite fair because of all that had happened to the nation and the field itself over the past decades. In 1900, for example, the Civil War was less history than a bad memory for the many Americans who had personally experienced it, and the frontier had famously just closed, according to Frederick Jackson Turner. The massive waves of immigration from eastern Europe and Russia were just beginning, and this was something that would irrevocably alter the nation's ethnic makeup and cultural identity. The Roaring Twenties, the Great Depression, and the New Deal resided in the future, of course, as did the rise of fascism and totalitarianism in Europe that now threatened America and its way of life. The United States was a world power, and an imperialist one at that, when the Japanese attacked Pearl Harbor, something that could not be said of the country when the USS *Maine* was sunk in Havana Harbor in 1898. In terms of both content and process, then, American history during World War II was much different from what it had been forty or even twenty years earlier, it is safe to say, with the last couple of generations making the subject a significantly more challenging one.[39]

## A Very Slight Acquaintance

The results of a study completed in 1943 were proof positive that all was not well in the United States when it came to American history. Collaborating with the Committee on American History in the Schools and Colleges, the *New York Times* surveyed seven thousand college freshmen to determine what they knew about the nation's past. The findings, which were widely reported in the media for decades to come, served as hard evidence that young people and American history were like strangers passing in the night. (The newspaper had already confirmed as much with a 1942 study that revealed that 82 percent of colleges in the United States did not require students to take any American history courses.[40]) The results of this second survey were nothing less than shocking. Of the freshmen, 25 percent did not know that Abraham Lincoln was president during the Civil War, and 84 percent could not cite two of Thomas Jefferson's achievements. More than two thousand of the seven thousand did not know Woodrow Wilson was president during the last world war, and almost half confused Andrew Jackson with Stonewall Jackson. When asked what Theodore Roosevelt's greatest contribution to the United States was, one student replied, "He collected large quantities of animal heads," an answer that was emblematic of the study's findings as a whole.[41]

These kinds of statistics and answers had an immediate effect on the country's education system. Committees were formed to study the problem, and grants were awarded to organizations committed to solving it. Proponents of social studies, a metafield that had begun to absorb American history in the 1920s by combining it with "current events," received a good part of the blame. States rushed to make American history compulsory in public high schools, and more scrutiny was directed at teachers of the subject.[42] "Too often, history courses are stepchildren in the country's schools," wrote Henry F. Pringle for the *Saturday Evening Post*, with school superintendents and principals thinking just about anybody could teach the subject if he or she just read from the textbook in class. (Gym teachers, notoriously, were sometimes assigned the task.) Some history classes mostly involved teachers leading a discussion based on stories in that day's newspaper, an approach that would obviously not equip students with the ability to answer difficult questions about events in the eighteenth and nineteenth centuries.[43]

Not surprisingly, the media had a field day with the story. "The younger generation of Americans has a very slight acquaintance with Clio [the muse of history], and no desire to improve it," noted the editors of *The Nation*, thinking the problem was mostly due to how the subject was taught. While the methodology of the study was clearly flawed (it appeared that some of the students applied a generous amount of adolescent humor in their choice of answers), there was enough in the findings to suggest that the Progressives' approach was leaving students with too little understanding of basic facts and the chronology of important events. Social content was being prioritized over the nuts and bolts of the subject as it used to be taught, critics asserted, the consequences of what they saw as a misguided, politically charged pedagogical approach now apparent. More generally, colleges and universities were not directing enough resources to American history (football coaches at large institutions were even then often paid more than professors of the subject), making the Progressives' agenda just part of the problem.[44]

The *New York Times* study crystallized what many had for some time felt about American history: that it was undertaught and underlearned. The American Historical Association took the news rather hard, blaming itself for not doing a better job in making the subject a priority among educators. Although such a claim was impossible to prove, many concluded that Americans knew less about their own history than at any other time, and this was an especially shocking revelation during wartime. Education in general had improved since the last world war, all agreed, but this begged the question of why American history had fallen behind. The simplest theory was that many students dropped out of high school before history was typically taught (in the junior and senior years), suggesting that the subject should be offered earlier. Because a common fluency in the subject was viewed as vital toward maintaining a democracy, however, strong emotions continued to swirl around the findings of the study. The Progressives were vilified in the press for their focus on the darker side of the American experience that had led students down the wrong path. For them, as historian Bernard Devoto put it in *Harper's*, "our civilization was low, our past ignoble, and our great men corrupt." It was a view that had distorted American history in the minds of young people or, perhaps even worse, made them uninterested in learning it.[45]

More than Progressives' less than sanguine take on American history contributed to college freshmen failing the *New York Times* quiz, however. Perhaps more than any other subject, Devoto believed, American history tried to "socialize" students via an attempt to infuse morality and ethics into what took place in the past. While well intended, the result was a perversion of history, reflecting the encroachment of the social sciences, and specifically sociology and psychology, into the field. As more humanitarian principles entered the equation, pure content—events, personalities, and experiences—dropped out, and this was the crux of the problem. Efforts to make history relevant were squeezing the real stuff of the past—dates, names, movements, wars, and political campaigns—out of classrooms, making it no surprise that students could not answer most of the questions asked by the newspaper. High school courses were "packed with goodwill but they have one unfortunate result—they produce illiteracy," Devoto concluded, calling for the American Historical Association to do whatever was in the organization's power to reform the field.[46]

Another problem with American history during the war, at least according to one scholar, was that it was too often taught and learned in a vacuum. This was especially true over the last couple of years, when both high schools and colleges introduced more American history classes in reaction to the alarming *New York Times* studies (and as a patriotic effort). For Eugene Byrne, a professor at Barnard, the dedicated approach to teaching American history was all wrong. Now, more than ever, the history of the United States should be seen from a global perspective, he (like Bolton) believed. This approach would be, Byrne argued, more in synch with the "de-isolation" of the country itself as it was forced to enter the war. In the fall of 1942, Byrne started teaching a course titled "World History from the American Standpoint, 1500–1942," challenging the accepted practice of presenting American history as a contained subject. Portraying the United States as an extension of European expansionism, a nation of immigrants, and as part of the "Americas" were all part of Byrne's method, as was emphasizing the role of people who helped put the country on an international stage (such as Benjamin Franklin and Woodrow Wilson). Students read books written not just by American authors but by citizens of other countries to get a better sense of how the United States had in the past been seen from abroad.[47]

Now, a year after the publication of his article in the *New York Times Magazine* in which he made a compelling argument that Americans should know their history, Allan Nevins could not resist again pleading his case in that same publication. The newspaper had completed and published the results of its history quiz over the course of that year, making the Columbia professor's warnings appear somewhat prescient. The findings of the survey spoke for themselves, he explained, and were a direct reflection of the education system's weakness when it came to American history. Although there were many causes for the flunking grade among college freshmen—too many subjects crowded into the high school curriculum, not enough time in the school day, poorly trained and overworked teachers, and some students' inability to remember facts—it was in the "confusion" within American history itself where most of the fault resided. It was, simply, unclear what should be taught and when, these fundamental unknowns making the students' poor showing almost expected.[48]

The "confusion" of American history had much to do with the hodgepodge nature of the nation's schools, Nevins believed. Rather than an organized whole, as in most European countries, American education was heavily state-based, a legacy of how the school system had developed over the past century or so. High schools were few and far between until the late nineteenth century and, until relatively recently, American history had been a subject dealing almost exclusively with political happenings. Things in the field became further "confused," Nevins continued, with the introduction of "progressive education" around the turn of the twentieth century. History's chronological and logical approach bumped directly into that of the social sciences, which was present-focused and thematic; it was a clash that marginalized the field and left it largely stranded in the sea of education. Better teachers, making courses in the subject mandatory for high school freshmen and sophomores, and keeping social studies (particularly the "current events" or "current affairs" component) distinct from American history were ways to add order to the field, Nevins suggested, thinking there was still cause for hope.[49]

Given how much attention was given to the *New York Times* history quiz for college freshmen, it was not surprising that the newspaper repeated it for different groups to test their knowledge of the subject. Again collaborating with its academic partner, the *Times* asked sixty-five questions to representative samples of people who presumably knew a good deal about American history. It was good news to learn that high school social studies teachers scored the highest on the test because they, of course, were responsible for educating the country's youth in the subject. Notably, a group from *Who's Who in America* finished second, suggesting a possible correlation between achievement and a familiarity with the nation's past. Editors of the *Times* could not resist posing a handful of the questions to its readers, no doubt wondering how conversant more average Americans were in the history of their country. By today's standards, the multiple-choice quiz was very difficult, with questions relating to seventeenth-century plantation owners, the first (1790) census, and the population of Indians at the time of the discovery of America by Europeans. Many readers no doubt flipped to page forty-six of the newspaper's magazine to find out how they did and were saddened to learn they knew no more about American history than the college students who had done poorly on the quiz.[50]

Were Americans truly historically illiterate? After studying the issue for a year, the Committee on American History in Schools and Colleges reported that while there was certainly a problem, it was not as bad as the media made it out to be. It was readily apparent that average Americans were not particularly good at recalling dates, names, or events, the committee conceded, but they understood the broad sweep of the nation's past and were aware of the contributions made by notable historical figures. In other words, knowledge of specific facts was less important than an appreciation for the symbolic value of our history, and this was a reasonable argument.[51] The war would soon be over, but Americans' problematic relationship with their country's history would not go away.

# 2   E Pluribus Unum

1946–1964

> His sense of the unity of America is largely unspecific and rests on a
> description of its multiplicity. His motto is e pluribus unum.
> John Higham, speaking of the typical consensus historian, 1962

On September 17, 1947, the Freedom Train left Philadelphia for a cross-country tour of the United States. The departure date and location were not randomly chosen. One hundred sixty years earlier on that day, in that city, the last session of the Federal Convention of 1787 was held, during which the U.S. Constitution was created. On board the train was a truly astounding collection of documents and flags, each artifact intended to convey the idea of freedom. A thirteenth-century copy of the Magna Carta was among the 126 documents, for example, as was an August 1945 log of the USS *Missouri* (which was the official site of the Japanese surrender of World War II).[1]

It was, however, the set of documents related to the founding of the nation that served as the centerpiece of the rolling exhibit. The Declaration of Independence (an early draft), the Articles of Confederation, the Constitution of 1787, and the Bill of Rights were on board, as was the Emancipation Proclamation. The Freedom Train would stop at each of the country's forty-eight states over the course of a year, something on which President Harry Truman himself insisted. Much attention was paid to the progress of the train as it chugged its way across the nation; it even became part of the adventures of the immensely popular *Li'l Abner* comic strip. The train and its message of freedom had a ripple effect throughout American society, especially in American education. Critical thinking was encouraged by integrating the nation's great documents into classroom materials, many high school teachers of American history found, as was a solid understanding of the country's political and economic structure.[2]

The Freedom Train and the enthusiastic reception it received from town to town were emblematic of the role of American history during the postwar years. Grounded in division and conflict in the 1920s and 1930s, the field took a sharp turn after World War II as the country settled into the domestic, consumer-oriented American way of life. Underlying the superficial tranquility, however, were real concerns and fears about a new and possibly more lethal threat: the spread of communism or even an atomic war. The Cold War was instrumental in forging the boundaries of American history from the late 1940s through the early 1960s, as the freedoms to be enjoyed in the United States were cast in high relief. Relatedly, Americans looked to their motto of unity through pluralism as an anchoring force, with this also heavily imprinting teaching and writing in the field.

## A Wider Knowledge of Who We Are

With the war emergency over, America had more time to reflect on its past. As the Freedom Train implied, the Allied victory over fascism and totalitarianism helped to bring out the nation's core values and raise the profile of history. As well, the new world order following the war was impetus for a wide variety of "experts" to urge Americans to know more about their history. Knowledge of history, especially one's own, was an ideal way to perpetuate the values and aspirations of a society; it was a way to make the past relevant. Rather than being dead and useless, then, American history was seen as a potentially vital force that could serve the interests of the nation and its people. Such a thing was especially important in the late 1940s, as postwar international relations became divisive along ideological lines. "No nation can manage its future which does not understand its past," stated Raymond B. Fosdick, president of the Rockefeller Foundation, in 1947, calling for "a wider knowledge of who we are and where and what we came from."[3] Others concurred that general fluency in American history could be a valuable asset in a troubled world. "It is knowledge of American history, in its broadest sense, that will guarantee an alert people," read an editorial in the *Annals of Iowa* in 1949, with such knowledge likely to create an awareness of "the loyalties, faiths, and ideals which are the driving forces of any happy and successful nation."[4] In short, a common understanding of American history could be a weapon in the escalating Cold War and, equally important, something that could discourage sympathy for socialist or communist ways of life on the domestic front.

Unfortunately, at least from the perspective of the more conservative, a good many of the intellectual elite appeared to be intrigued by socialism and communism after the war, a supposed direct result of the failures of American education. Even then, colleges were commonly viewed as a breeding ground of anticapitalist thought, with young people's minds shaped by radical professors critical of the American way of life. One person in particular was blamed for these "unwholesome" political attitudes: Charles A. Beard. Although the man was in the final year of his life in 1948, his work from decades earlier continued to reverberate through the hallowed halls of university history departments. According to critics, it was, specifically, Beard's 1913 book *An Economic Interpretation of the Constitution of the United States* that did the most damage to the Founding Fathers and the documents they forged. Rather than declaring independence for the benefit of all the people, Beard had proposed, the mostly wealthy men were looking out for their own economic interests and those of a similar privileged class. Debunking the Founding Fathers' motives was a prime example of the theory of "economic determinism," the idea that people did things in the pursuit of personal gain versus collective good. When applied to the founding of the United States, economic determinism obviously became much more than an interesting theory. Offering a different interpretation of the intent of the signers of the Declaration of Independence and framers of the Constitution challenged the accepted beliefs regarding the origins of the country and posed a significant threat to the fundamental principles that guided the nation.[5]

Beard's book, which was often assigned in collegiate history classes between the wars, heavily imprinted American education into the late 1940s. The Building America series of high school textbooks, for example, was clearly inspired by Beard's thinking, much to the chagrin of those on the right: they deemed Beard and his colleagues at Columbia University to be intellectual descendants of Karl Marx, and by extension believed that communist theories were in active circulation in the nation's schools. (While Beard did rely heavily upon Marxist analysis, he was not in fact a communist sympathizer, a distinction many Cold War ultra-conservatives did not make; Marxist theory or ideology was quite different from the system of communism in action, another important distinction that was sometimes overlooked by those leaning heavily toward the right.) Graduates of Teachers College at Columbia further spread the gospel of Beard and some of his colleagues (notably, John Dewey); these self-described "frontier thinkers" were accused of disseminating subversive doctrines under the guise of "liberalism" or "progressive education." All this was, according to ultraconservatives, a carefully orchestrated plan by communist sympathizers to turn the very building blocks of American exceptionalism into an elaborate expression of avarice and materialism. Postwar teachers of American history were assigned the responsibility to reverse this stream of dangerous thinking by returning to the original beliefs regarding the formation of the nation that were so firmly entrenched in our public memory.[6]

In fact, in many states through the postwar years, it was required for high school classes in American history to include a study of communism or, more accurately, anticommunism. American history was a likely subject in which to instill nationalistic values among teenagers, a pursuit that almost guaranteed that our way of life would be (favorably) contrasted with that of the Soviets during the Cold War. While the power and influence of the House Un-American Activities Committee had much to do with the anticommunism fervor, the Red Scare and pro-Americanism derived from many sources and were driven by the powers that be rather than happening spontaneously. No sympathy for—or even a full understanding of—communism was typically tolerated in many school districts, as right-wing groups pressured administrators to take a strictly "patriotic" approach in teaching the topic. Ironically, such classes became a tutorial in propaganda versus an example of objective analysis, and this was precisely the opposite of the original intent. Teachers were strongly encouraged to show in class the film *Communism on the Map*, which (incorrectly) depicted the virulent spread of communism around the world, and strongly discouraged from screening the award-winning *Face of Red China* because it included shots of smiling Chinese children (implying they were happy under communist rule, contrary to what the Right liked to believe).[7]

America's obsession with communism, particularly as it played out in the nation's classrooms, was all the more unfortunate given that there were obvious, gaping holes in the teaching of our own history. The first half of American history was especially neglected in academic circles in the late 1940s, making the reaffirmation of faith in the beginnings of the American idea and experience all the more challenging. College-level courses in the colonial or Revolutionary War eras were surprisingly scarce, even in parts of the country with a rich heritage in that period, and high schoolers spent precious little time studying the remarkable events that had taken place over the course of that century or so. In addition, little new scholarship dedicated to the era was being published, and this, too, was rather strange given the era's prominent place in the popular imagination. Notably, generous amounts of space had been devoted to the seventeenth and eighteenth centuries in American history textbooks before 1920, making the current lack of attention to the period all the more conspicuous. Interest in nineteenth-century topics like Western expansion and slavery, and twentieth-century movements and programs such as the New Deal, were clearly stealing much of the colonial era's thunder, as the former were generally viewed as more relevant to the economic and political complexities of postwar everyday life.[8]

Paradoxically, history in the colonial and Revolutionary War eras was remarkably popular among a general audience. Books about the period by historians such as Carl Van Doren and James Truslow Adams were selling well, and biographies of Benjamin Franklin and Paul Revere had recently won the Pulitzer Prize. Historical novels set in colonial days were also being eagerly published and read, some hitting the best seller list. Alongside this literary interest in the formative years of the United States was a surge in membership in "patriotic societies" like the Daughters of the American Revolution and its male counterpart. Additionally, sites such as Concord, Jamestown, Morristown, Ticonderoga, Valley Forge, and Yorktown were popular tourism destinations, and Colonial Williamsburg allowed visitors to experience American life as it was in the late eighteenth century. Museums were actively collecting and exhibiting art and artifacts from the period, and neocolonial architecture was frequently popping up in the new suburbs being built, in the retail arena, and on university campuses. Hollywood had also caught the colonial bug, with period films set during or around the Revolutionary War (such as Abbott and Costello's wonderful 1946 *The Time of Their Lives*) and creating a genre unto itself. "Indications of a widespread popular interest in early American history are abundant," noted Carl Bridenbaugh in the *American Historical Review* in 1948, wondering why academics were far less intrigued by the era.[9]

Teachers of American history in the postwar years faced challenges that went far beyond the neglect of the late 1700s. Midcentury educators were unsure of the best method by which to teach the subject, will little research done to support or exclude any particular approach. Something teachers could agree on was that any and all pedagogical methods should instill some sort of values in the student. Most American high school students did not go on to college at the time (just one in seven did; another one in seven enrolled in a nursing program or trade school), meaning preparation for higher education was typically not the goal. At the time, the purpose of education in general was seen as to shape the behavior of young people in a "desirable" fashion. Specifically, American history was considered an ideal subject to help future adults in a social sense; the field was thus viewed as much more than the acquisition of facts about the past. A solid grasp of American history "will result in better behavior, conduct, or action than ignorance or lack of understanding of them will do," wrote James A. Boyd, a teacher at Newton High School in Newtonville, Massachusetts, in the *School Review* in 1950. The positive values of tolerance, social consciousness, sympathy, cooperation, and responsibility could all be developed by a greater comprehension of the nation's history, Boyd and many other teachers believed, and the field could be a kind of platform for good citizenship.[10]

While the *what* was considered much more important than the *how*, a group of American history high school teachers in another part of the country did have some opinions on the methods of teaching the subject. Five teachers at Battle Creek High School in Michigan had an interesting theory about American history and the role it could play among young people, as they subsequently wrote in the *School Review* in 1951. "If boys and girls can be taught to develop a reasoning admiration for outstanding American historical personages," they proposed, "they will, to a measurable degree, incorporate into their own behavior patterns some of the outstanding desirable characteristics of these same historic personages." By absorbing some of the positive traits of our "great men" (all of the twenty-eight selected were white men except Harriet B. Stowe), the idea went, America's youth would, in some way and at some level, be great themselves.[11]

Clearly excited about such a prospect, the teachers decided to test their idea by emphasizing a biographic approach in their American history classes. Via films, novels, and other materials, students learned about the lives of the twenty-eight notable figures of the eighteenth and nineteenth centuries. The team then tried to determine if knowledge about people like Benjamin Franklin, Andrew Jackson, Thomas Jefferson, Robert E. Lee, and Daniel Webster translated into admiration for them. (Admiration was viewed as an indicator that students would adopt some of their characteristics, a tenuous supposition at best.) Regardless, little correlation was found between knowledge and admiration, leaving no real answers about whether the popular biographical method of teaching the history of the United States could help produce the "greatest generation" of Americans.[12]

## The Crisis of the Present

American history was assigned a still greater duty in the years following World War II. Major social, political, and economic events often served as an opportune time to look back to parallel situations of the past in order to add context and perspective, and this was especially true in the anxious 1950s. The Cold War stirred American historians to report what statesmen of a century or two earlier did during their own international crises in the hope that some valuable learnings could be gleaned and perhaps applied. For example, in his 1950 essay "Early Cold Wars" in

*Current History*, Gale W. McGee, a professor of history at the University of Wyoming, pointed out that the Founding Fathers were hardly the resolute isolationists many believed them to be. Political leaders of the late eighteenth and early nineteenth centuries knew that creating alliances with foreign countries could be a valuable agent of national security, thus making the then current international deal-making not so unusual or alarming. "The Founding Fathers did not try to escape the responsibilities of their own cold war," McGee wrote, noting that they, too, were aware that getting involved in European political machinations was sometimes necessary in order to keep the peace. Getting mixed up in the affairs of the Old World was not unusual, in other words, a revelation to those thinking that our participation in the North Atlantic Treaty Organization would cause George Washington to roll over in his grave. Comparing the political dynamics of the cold wars of yesterday and today was a good example of how knowledge of the past could be a valuable resource for the present.[13]

The political scandals of the early 1950s were also cause for historians to parse the past for comparable events. Some believed that public officials taking bribes, awarding lucrative defense contracts in return for political favors, or partnering with organized crime—as dozens were alleged to have recently done—was something new. Again, however, this was not the case, with corruption within the federal government a running theme throughout our history (sadly enough). In a pair of essays in *Current History* in 1952, Sidney Warren described how corrupt politics and politicians were in antebellum days, and especially during the administration of President Ulysses S. Grant. Given the crooked ways of the past, there was little reason to be shocked or outraged about the reported shenanigans in Washington DC, Warren explained, or to be concerned that the moral fiber of the nation had been shredded. Public officials using their power for personal gain was as old a story as politics itself, one could reasonably conclude—something that should almost be expected (though not tolerated).[14]

Other historians of the Cold War era found comfort in the fact that the nation had survived many crises of the past. America and Americans had run the gauntlet of challenges over the past two centuries, Henry

Steele Commager reminded readers of the *New York Times* in 1953, evidence that suggested the country and its citizens could endure the then current communist threat. The battles of the Revolutionary War, and keeping a vast, territorial nation together after that war, the Civil War, the Great Depression, and the attack on Pearl Harbor were just some of the major challenges we had faced and, needless to say, overcome. In fact, in the spirit of Friedrich Nietzsche's famous quote, "That which does not kill us makes us stronger," Commager argued that such crises had made us a tougher, more resilient people. Our core practices and principles—democratic government, commitment to freedom, adaptability, and refusal to panic—were the primary reasons why the country had not just survived over the years but thrived. "Seen in historical perspective there is nothing unprecedented or ominous about the crisis of the present," Commager concluded, not especially worried that the United States would be brought down or destroyed by a foreign power.[15]

Popular culture mining the (mythical) past also served as a vehicle to soothe Americans' nerves during the Cold War. The "Wild West" was a prime locale for movies of the postwar era, and these shoot-'em-ups were not just entertainment but metaphors for the battle between the American way of life and the communist system. (The equally popular "alien invasion" genre served the same role.) Historical Westerns like *Red River* (1948), *Shane* (1953), *Gunfight at the O.K. Corral* (1957), and *Rio Bravo* (1959) were films that offered an uncomplicated interpretation of the conflict between the good guys (us) and the bad guys (them). (John Ford's *The Searchers* of 1956, on the other hand, was filled with ambiguities.) The nineteenth-century West was, of course, also a visible presence on the new medium of television. *Bonanza, Gunsmoke, Have Gun—Will Travel, The Lone Ranger,* and *Rawhide* were tremendously popular shows despite or because of their white-hat-versus-black-hat simplicity, making Americans feel good that they were on the right side of the Cold War. Much of these shows' popularity also resided in the fact that there were only a few networks at the time, resulting in extremely high ratings versus the more than five hundred channels we have today. Because it reached millions of viewers, the legitimately mass medium of early television exposed more people to American history than ever before, one could argue, even if shows like *The Lone Ranger* or *Bat Masterson* were significantly less than historically accurate.[16]

It was not a television show, however, but Walt Disney's interpretation of the past, particularly the nineteenth-century West, that most ingeniously captured Americans' imaginations—particularly those of young people. Opening in 1955, Disneyland in Anaheim, California, offered visitors a kaleidoscopic trip through time and space, something that instantly made it the most popular theme park in the world (a claim held to this day). Two of the park's original five themed "lands" were historical in nature, drawing upon the appeal of the mythical American past in the mid-1950s. Main Street U.S.A. was one of these, a highly stylized replica of a "typical" Midwest town of the early twentieth century. Visitors who did not enter the park by monorail were immediately transported to Main Street U.S.A., where they encountered Victorian-era versions of a train station, town square, movie theater, city hall, firehouse, and shops. Main Street U.S.A. was clearly inspired by Disney's childhood in Marceline, Missouri (and that of his colleague Harper Goff, who grew up in Fort Collins, Colorado), offering visitors a nostalgic (and scaled-down) walk through a more innocent and—many no doubt believed—happier time.

While certainly entertaining as a kind of simulated time capsule, Main Street U.S.A. was just the beginning of one's journey through America's largely fabricated past. Before or after taking in the exotic Adventureland, dreamy Fantasyland, or futuristic Tomorrowland, visitors entered Frontierland, where they had the chance to relive what was presented as America's "pioneer days." With animatronic Native Americans (the "Pinewood Indians"), the Big Thunder Mountain Railroad, the Mark Twain Riverboat, the Sailing Ship *Columbia*, the Pirate's Lair on Tom Sawyer Island, and the Shootin' Exposition, Frontierland was a crazy concoction of nineteenth-century Western iconography. A trip to Frontierland would not have been complete without moseying over to the Golden Horseshoe Saloon and its revue featuring Old West–style entertainment (which ran for three decades before being revamped). A real stagecoach pulled by horses, a Conestoga wagon, a set of pack mules, a train ride through a mine, Indian war canoes, and an Indian village were also part of

Frontierland, which was (and continues to be) one of the most popular areas of the park.

Another original, short-lived feature of Frontierland was the Davy Crockett Museum, which included vignettes (and related merchandise) from Disney's *Davy Crockett* television series. *Davy Crockett*, based on the real-life frontiersman, soldier, and politician who became a folk hero after his death at the Battle of the Alamo in 1836, was in fact a primary reason Disneyland existed in the first place. Walt Disney was able to make his ambitious dream possible by building his huge park after agreeing with ABC to produce a weekly, one-hour television series based on the exciting life of Crockett. Disney made five episodes of the show that aired from December 1954 to December 1955: "Davy Crockett, Indian Fighter"; "Davy Crockett Goes to Congress"; "Davy Crockett at the Alamo"; "Davy Crockett's Keelboat Race"; and "Davy Crockett and the River Pirates." (The first three episodes were put together as the 1955 feature film *Davy Crockett, King of the Wild Frontier*, and the latter two as *Davy Crockett and the River Pirates*, which was released the following year.) Sticking to the known facts about Crockett's life, need it be said, was not a priority for Disney's team, something critics at the time duly noted.

Such voices of criticism were lost in the din of wild (and largely unanticipated) success, however. Much in part due to its catchy theme song, "The Ballad of Davy Crockett" ("Born on a mountainside in Tennessee / Greenest state in the land of the free"), the show was an immediate hit. More important (or at least more profitable), millions of copies of the record were sold, and all kinds of show-related merchandise—clothes, toy rifles and knives, books, and almost everything else in which a young baby boomer would be interested—flew off the shelves. "Coonskin hats" were a particular favorite, turning the show into a true cultural phenomenon. Not just kids but a good number of adults were drawn to the show, as the production values were superior to almost everything else on the air at the time. The series even sparked a political row, with liberals and conservatives debating the character of the real-life Davy Crockett. What was behind the *Davy Crockett* phenomenon? In *Walt Disney: The Triumph of the American Imagination*, Neal Gabler posed a compelling theory. "Walt Disney had clearly struck a national nerve, even if accidentally, in reviving the idea of a plainspoken, fearless, idealistic, compassionate, but intrepid hero, at a time when Americans were harking back to values that they believed distinguished them from the conformity and cold-bloodedness of their global antagonist, the Soviet Union," he wrote, portraying the show as a resounding retort to communism. While thinking they were just playing cowboys and Indians, boys and girls in coonskin hats might very well have been doing their part to win the Cold War.[17]

## Our Long Look Backward

Pretending to be Wyatt Earp while sipping a root beer at the Golden Horseshoe Saloon was undoubtedly loads of fun, but American history was typically a more complicated affair in the 1950s. During the Korean War, for example, captors grilled American prisoners of war (POWs) in order to determine what the latter knew about the political landscape of the United States, both past and present. The Koreans and Chinese were taken aback by how little the American soldiers knew about their own history; in fact, the enemy was often more well versed in the nation's past than were the POWs. "They couldn't answer the arguments in favor of Communism with arguments in favor of Americanism," read a 1956 Defense Department prisoner of war report, "because they knew very little about their America."[18]

This was hardly the only indication that adults in this country were not especially fluent in American history. One recent survey showed that despite the much-publicized Freedom Train promotion, many Americans lacked a familiarity with the primary documents of the country's founding; one-third of those interviewed were unacquainted with the Bill of Rights. "All this points inescapably to our failure to inculcate in a significant segment of our people the basic elements of American history," wrote W. Harwood Huffcut in the Saturday Evening Post. Huffcut believed that much of the humanity and emotion had been extracted from the subject and that this explained why Americans knew less about their own history than did foreign enemies. "It is time to make our history and our traditions glow and throb again," he declared, calling for the country's educational system to put "the heart and soul" back into the subject.[19]

The Korean POW incident could be said to have been the tipping point with regard to the apparent letdown of American history during the Cold War. Critics asked who had failed the young men in their lack of familiarity with the fundamental foundation of the American way of life, wondering if it was home, school, the church, or community at large. Because their nation's history was an important element of citizenship, Americans should learn it at an early age, experts in such things reemphasized, putting more pressure on teachers of the subject at the elementary school level. New resources, such as a booklet published by the American Association of School Administrators in 1956, were developed to help educators achieve this ambitious goal. Every child should attain "an enduring body of memories about the personalities [and] the achievements of the men and women who have built the United States of America," the booklet advised educators, adding that all citizens should have "a strong emotional devotion to the ideals we cherish as a nation." Against the backdrop of the Cold War, the country's educational system was assigned the mission to instill pride in America's past, something that was essential to developing patriotic citizens. Schools had the responsibility to teach not just the ABCs but the love of one's country, in other words, a mighty task that had seemingly gone largely ignored.[20]

In one sense it was puzzling why young people were not conversant in American history. The country spent more money on education than any other, for one thing, and the subject was taught in virtually every public school in the nation. More students were taking courses in American history than ever before, in fact, and this suggested that adolescents should have at least a basic understanding of the subject. One could possibly conclude that American students were just not very smart, but this was not even considered. Instead, the two most obvious factors— textbooks and teachers—were put to blame, and most concluded that neither was offering students enough critical thinking. The top textbooks were unarguably uniform and homogeneous, as too much money was at stake for publishers to develop anything truly different from the norm. In addition, the books were typically weighted heavily toward events of the past two decades, a result of the common thinking that most students had little interest in anything that happened before they were born. Pages dedicated to the American Revolution and Founding Fathers remained surprisingly few—fewer, in fact, than the number usually allotted to Franklin Delano Roosevelt or his New Deal.[21]

Although the balance of American history textbooks was certainly not ideal, it was the books' utter middle-of-the-roadness that so riled critics. Taking any particular side in a controversial historical event was risky from a business sense because a school district might drop the book, and this was reason enough for publishers to present opposing sides on any politically charged issue. The problem with this approach was that it inevitably watered down interesting sites of American history such as the New Deal. Saying something partisan would have been better than saying nothing at all, some felt, as the former would at least make students think. Instead, students were apt to read the material on automatic pilot, knowing there would be nothing in the books with which to strongly agree or disagree. Neutrality of thought and sweeping generalizations filled the books, thought people like George Rudisill, a professor at Wayne State University, and there was no mention of provocative but important topics such as birth control, the military, or crime. Be brief, stay close to the facts, and make history entertaining were the basic three rules of publishing textbooks, one might conclude after reading a few, and it was a formula that may have been financially successful but was failing to teach students anything significant about the subject. "American history has simply become another commodity to be peddled in a protected market, its determined by the size of sales rather than by any intrinsic merit of the product itself," Rudisill concluded after thorough analysis.[22]

It was obvious to some that the country's education system could not be relied upon to teach young people what they should know about American history. With the subject cast as nothing less than a matter of national security, parents were encouraged to make American history an engaging dimension of their children's upbringing. "Spring and summer weather make jaunts about the countryside, visits to historical shrines, and to famous battlefields and landmarks an appealing family enterprise," wrote Dorothy Barclay in the New York Times in 1956, thinking such field trips could "stimulate much good talk about the meaning of the events of the past." Young children might find historic homes especially interesting, she believed, because of the natural urge to compare toys, beds, and clothes of the past with their own. Barclay reported that one family had recently visited the Theodore Roosevelt House at Sagamore Hill, New York, after which an art project was assigned. The children made drawings illustrating the man's great achievements in both peace and war, and it was a perfect way, in Barclay's words, to "make our history come alive." A basic understanding of American history could be gained from teachers and textbooks, Barclay and others believed, but it was parents who could and should make the subject exciting.[23]

Others agreed that it was outside the classroom where the measure of American history should be judged. "There are signs today that Americans are more mindful of their national history than they used to be," wrote Dumas Malone for the New York Times just a month after Barclay's article appeared, taking a much different tack from that of critics of the education system. Malone, a professor of history at Columbia University, also had a significantly different view of the architects of the nation from those who taught at the very same department a generation earlier. Malone, a scholar specializing in Jefferson, was pleased by the populist appeal of the Founding Fathers and was not at all bothered by the lack of scholarly material dedicated to them nor interested in "debunking" the myths surrounding the men. With sites such as Monticello, Mount Vernon, and Williamsburg frequent stops on family car trips, it did indeed appear that Americans were curious about the country's mythic past. Little of the bashing of the "Fathers of the republic" so prevalent in the first half of the century could be detected, and this was a major turnaround in the field. Widely viewed during the period between the wars as a profit-minded elite, the men were now increasingly seen as models of leadership through their realization of an independent nation and formation of a democratic government bound by the Constitution. Time had served the men well, Malone believed, and their achievements were now considered far more remarkable than they had been at the beginning of the twentieth century. Since then our principles had stood the test of two world wars and the Great Depression, additional evidence of how sound the Founding Fathers' ideas really were.[24]

There was, however, more to the popularization of colonial American history in the 1950s, Malone proposed. "One reason for our long look backward may be that a bewildered and beleaguered society like ours, feeling insecure in the present and unsure of the future, is seeking to tap the wisdom and experience of the Fathers," he suggested, implying that there was perhaps nowhere better to look for guidance as we clashed with another superpower. Malone even played a "What Would the Founding Fathers Do?" game, offering his thoughts on the role some of the men would play or what they would advise if facing the challenges of the present day. George Washington, for example, would urge that the nation, and especially political parties and special interest groups, remain united when confronting foreign threats; Benjamin Franklin would, naturally, hold a diplomatic post (ideally in France) or perhaps represent the country as a United Nations delegate; John Adams would serve in the U.S. Congress but, because of his gruffness with colleagues, offer the greatest contribution as a sort of a modern day philosopher; James Madison would make a great legislator in Congress with his unsurpassed ability to balance the need for a strong government with individual liberties; and Thomas Jefferson—given his disdain for politicking—would likely accept a high-appointed office, perhaps that of secretary of state (a position he had actually held). Alexander Hamilton, meanwhile, would be better off in business than politics, Malone contended, a good candidate for president of General Motors or U.S. Steel but not well suited for public office.[25]

## People of Plenty

By the end of the 1950s it was readily apparent that American history had changed a great deal over the previous decade and a half. Beard's Progressive view grounded in economic determinism had finally run out of steam, much to the delight of more conservative critics. In fact, the standing of the three giants of the field in the 1920s and 1930s—Beard, Frederick Jackson Turner, and Vernon Louis Parrington—had all shrunk considerably as their fundamental interpretation of the nation's past centered around the idea of conflict fell out of favor. (Carl Becker, a student of Turner's, was another key figure in the school, his work also no longer considered a must-read in the field.) While the struggle between the "common man" and a privileged elite was no doubt a huge part of the American story, it was no longer viewed as fresh or positive enough to engage the current crop of historians. For the latter, the between-the-wars version of American history was too disjointed and conflict oriented, with Progressives overly concerned with the continual jockeying for power among groups with opposing ideologies.[26]

Now, in these more conservative times, it was a traditional and conformist view of the nation's past to which American historians were most attracted. Inspired by Alexis de Tocqueville and his homogeneous depiction of the young country, contemporary historians were keen on, in John Higham's words, "smooth[ing] over America's social convulsions." Writing in *Commentary* in 1959, Higham described what was referred to as the consensus school of American history as a "cult," its adherents reading events and movements as illustrative of stability and harmony versus turmoil and upheaval. One of the new giants of the field, Richard Hofstadter, had recently argued that late nineteenth-century populism and early twentieth-century Progressivism were less revolutionary movements than had commonly been believed, espousing an almost nostalgic view of the past. Notably, as with the colonial or Revolutionary War eras, general readers were quite fascinated with the telling of stories about the Civil War but scholars were largely avoiding the subject, perhaps because it presented too mighty a task to smooth over. (Another top consensus historian, Daniel Boorstin, arguably achieved it with his *The Americans: The National Experience*.) Continuity, holism, and unity defined "the American experience," consensus historians held, and the often-used phrase itself emphasized commonality over discord.[27]

Consensus historians differed from scholars of the previous generation in other important respects. If conflict was the central theme of the Progressive American historians of the 1920s and 1930s, those of the postwar years were equally enamored of the idea of our "national character." Americans were a unique people, the latter firmly believed, our differences less important than what we had in common. David Potter's 1954 *People of Plenty: Economic Abundance and the American Character* was a perfect example of how a contemporary historian had used the idea of commonality to tell the American story, in this case through an economic lens. A book like *People of Plenty* could never have been written between the wars, it is safe to say, as historians of that period would find both the idea of a single "people" or general state of "plentitude" alien concepts. While Higham acknowledged that "important and original work" was coming out of the consensus school, he had major concerns about its limitations. "The conservative frame of reference creates a paralyzing incapacity to deal with the elements of spontaneity, effervescence, and violence in American history," he posited, thinking that even the best practitioners of the day were playing it a bit too safe. The United States may not have been as divided as Progressives contended, but viewing the nation's past through rose-colored glasses, as consensus historians did, was equally misguided.[28]

Consensus historians were, of course, not operating in a vacuum; it was clear to all that the postwar pressures of conformity and homogeneity had a direct impact on how they approached American history. A generation earlier, the field was heavily shaped by what could be called cultural pluralism—that is, examples of regional, class, and ethnic differences—as many Americans pushed back against the rising tide of modernity and national standardization. (It is worth noting that something not unlike this would happen again a generation later.) Historians then often wrote about the past from their own, typically personal perspective, the resultant book or essay a treatise of sorts for one's particular version of national identity. Little of that was being done in the 1950s and early 1960s, the group loyalties of historians having broken down. With the Progressive view of American history similarly eroded, the orientation of the field further shifted, making it almost hard to recognize from a pre-war perspective. Continual improvement and betterment—disrupted by the occasional reversal—was no longer the central theme of American history. The Progressive focus on conflict had by the early 1960s almost disappeared, a startling reversal over the course of just a couple of decades. Likewise, the nation's past had ceased to be a story of struggle among groups divided economically, geographically, or ideologically. American history was now for the most part a story of shared aims and collective interests, and this was something that would be virtually unrecognizable (and abhorrent) to Beard, Turner, Parrington, or their followers.[29]

A growing consciousness of being part of an international community during the postwar era also played a significant role in this transformation of the field. When cast alongside the Cold War and defense of the domestic, consumer-oriented American way of life, a grand narrative of national progress did indeed appear less convincing. Continuity took precedence over change, a key marker of conservative values. "Many historians now emphasized the enduring uniformities of American life, the stability of institutions, and the persistence of a national character," Higham wrote in 1962, and the consensus school was now, more than ever, the dominant view in the field. Amazingly, the division (and sometimes antipathy) between political parties and ideologies that was so much a part of American history—Left versus Right, liberal versus conservative, Democrat versus Republican—shrank considerably under the pressure of the consensus. Such differences were simply alternative expressions of the same basic idea, postwar historians argued, a prime example of how resistant to conflict this school of thought could be.[30]

With *The Reconstruction of American History*, a collection of essays published that same year, Higham illustrated the degree to which the field had been transformed since World War II. As editor of the book, Higham chose essays that revealed how interpretations of basic topics in American history had been significantly altered over the past generation.[31] It could not be argued that the change was not dramatic. Over the course of a couple of decades, the Puritans had morphed from rebellious zealots to kind philosophers; the American Revolution was no longer a radical break from an oppressive ruler but instead the final stage of an evolving political process; Jacksonian democracy was less a sweeping reform movement than an exercise in capitalism; and the robber barons of the Gilded Age were not greedy thieves but instead savvy entrepreneurs. Could anything once accepted to be true about American history still be believed?[32]

## The Elders of Our Tribe

As the quantity of writings of American history accelerated in the late 1950s and early 1960s, the answer to that question was increasingly "no." The field had not only shifted course but was now expanding rapidly, making the postwar years a heyday of American history. "We are entering a new phase in the study of the American past," proclaimed Leo Marx, a professor of English at Amherst College, in 1961, genuinely thrilled at the recent outpouring of scholarly material dedicated to the nation's history. Indeed, new volumes on Ralph Waldo Emerson and Thomas Jefferson had just appeared, as had a massive anthology on what the publisher called "the development of American life and thought," an obviously ambitious undertaking.[33] The papers of Benjamin Franklin, John Adams, Alexander Hamilton, and James Madison were also now on bookshelves, making up for the relative lack of attention to colonial-era history over the past couple of decades. This outpouring of material dedicated to the nation's founding was not a coincidence. At the Library of Congress back in 1950, President Truman was presented with the first volume of *The Papers of Thomas Jefferson*, and the rest, one could say, was history. Upon accepting the book, Truman, an avid reader of American history, asked the National Historical Publications Commission to make available "the writings of men whose contributions to our history are now inadequately represented by published works." More such works rolled off the presses over the next decade, fulfilling the president's dream of putting into print the primary documents of the American Enlightenment.[34]

Many more big projects were in the works in the early 1960s, making it an exhilarating time for both American history and American studies, the latter taking an interdepartmental or multidisciplinary approach. Although the initiative had begun a dozen years earlier, the excitement surrounding the administration of President John F. Kennedy appeared to be contributing to the renewed interest in the origins of the American idea and experience. Ardent supporters of Kennedy saw the man and his bold vision of the future as aligned with those of the Founding Fathers, making the publication of the latter's original writings highly relevant given the challenges of the day, both domestic and foreign. Adrienne Koch, professor of American studies at the University of California, was positively ecstatic about the new literary genre that had been created and how it could be used to spread freedom and equality around the world. Consistent with one of JFK's favorite phrases, the body of work would ideally serve as an instrument not just for looking back but to "move forward": "These writings do indeed promise to transform American history; to give to the reading part of the American people the means to win back the legacy that the farsighted founding statesmen were concerned to give them; and they will exert an invaluable influence on the world-wide evaluation of American civilization, the character of its great leaders, and the contribution of American philosopher-statesmen to political thought and institutions."[35]

Others welcomed the new, much overdue attention to the work of "the elders of our tribe," as David L. Norton put it. Norton, who taught at the Ethical Society of St. Louis, believed that our collective ignorance of history in general was "a congenital defect in our culture," an innate and unfortunate trait. "By temperament forward-looking, we Americans have been unconsciously careless of our past," he wrote in 1961 in *The Nation*, noting that our focus on each new day made us quickly forget what happened the day before. Outside the academic arena history was for the most part a hobby, with enthusiasts attending meetings at their local historical societies or perhaps retracing the steps of soldiers on Civil War battlegrounds. It was true that we celebrated Washington's birthday every February, but much of what we knew about the man was steeped in mythology versus truth. (The account of his chopping down a cherry tree and then confessing the misdeed to his father was in all likelihood a fabrication to teach children the principle of honesty.) The publication of the Founding Fathers' papers was thus the ideal way to correct this wrong, Norton felt, the output and detail of the material truly amazing given how long it had lain dormant. Not just speeches, essays, letters, memoranda, grants, and writs were being published but, in some cases, the great men's checkbook entries and laundry lists—the latter offering a different, and sometimes keener, kind of insight into character. Best of all, while scholars would likely benefit most from the new publications, lay readers would also have easy access to the works. The prefaces and introductions to the multivolume sets were in fact written for a general audience, a conscious step designed to bring "real" American history to the American people.[36]

It was not just the quantity of new, colonial-era material that pleased Leo Marx, Adrienne Koch, and many other scholars but also the quality. The style of presenting American history was changing, Marx felt, taking the field further into uncharted territory. "If I had to choose a single name for the emerging style it would be one of the following: documentary, objective, professional, organized, or official," he proposed, the field reflecting the more scientific approach being taken within academia and in society as a whole. For decades, American history was the realm of independent intellectuals with interesting ideas but often arcane ways of presenting their material; the field was now becoming more systematic, which was a common practice in the bureaucracy-obsessed postwar years.[37]

Was there any downside to this new, more methodical style of American history? Potentially so, Marx believed. More scholars were working in teams, for one thing, part of large projects funded by private organizations (such as the Rockefeller Foundation) or corporations. The government was often involved in some way in these efforts, further diminishing the role and/or responsibility of the individual. Most "humanists" were not used to working within such an institutional environment, Marx pointed out, raising possible red flags. He wondered if American history should be so "precise, neutral, and impersonal." Would self-expression be left out of such a research-driven process? American history was not intended to be "predictable, safe, and sound," he argued, noting that the best scholarship was often disturbing to some. Turning the humanities into purely empirical disciplines would be a big mistake, Marx warned, with the need to "put the pieces together" unchanged. True scholars, he concluded, should continue to endow data "with meaning and value by framing it within the largest context," this being the real job of the "fully engaged intellectual."[38]

## This Powerful Moral Imperative

While American history was becoming more professional, the field had a long way to go in its treatment of African Americans in textbooks. The "integration" of American history textbooks was an interesting aspect of the civil rights movement that has gone largely ignored. With standard textbooks in the field focusing on the actions of white, Anglo Saxon, Protestant men, Negro History Week and history clubs were the only real opportunities for discussing the role of African Americans in any detail. (Negro History Week was created in 1926 by Carter G. Woodson and the

Association for the Study of Negro Life and History; it morphed into Black History Month in 1976.) Encyclopedias were another source of contention. Most teachers in predominantly African American communities used the materials that were readily available because they were not sure what else they could do (or nervous about losing their jobs should they rock the boat). Teachers understood that African American history should not be treated as a separate subject but, in the parlance of the day, "correlated" with American history. Josie Lawrence, a high school teacher in Montgomery, Alabama, was keenly aware that it was important that history not be segregated as it routinely was in the United States in the 1950s. "We may talk about respect, race, pride, and heritage, but until we place in the high schools a correlation of Negro History with American History our children's attitudes will have formed which are inferior and that the color of their skin is a basic factor," she told members of the Association for the Study of Negro Life and History in 1958. Fortunately, Lawrence had discovered some useful materials written by colleagues in Missouri and was using them as a supplement in her class to "correlate" the two histories.[39]

One of the reasons American history textbooks had to be revised was simply that more African Americans were going to and staying in school. Widespread changes in the country's educational landscape were thus operating alongside the hard-fought struggle to desegregate the American public school system that took place as part of the civil rights movement. American education was heavily racially divided prior to 1954 when, via *Brown v. Board of Education*, the U.S. Supreme Court made segregation of public schools unconstitutional. Prior to the landmark case, nonwhites were systemically excluded from the national imagination, and negative racial stereotypes routinely appeared in textbooks. In addition, most professional historians harbored traditional interpretations of slavery, the Civil War, and Reconstruction up to that time, all of these practices products of deep-seated racial prejudice rather than mere oversight by myopic scholars.

By the late 1950s, however, American education was becoming less exclusionary, and thus the materials used in classrooms had to become more pluralistic. Textbooks in higher education were a particular concern,

as it was colleges and universities that would churn out the next generation of teachers. There was also a growing awareness that textbooks were
written exclusively for young people growing up within a white-oriented
culture. African Americans often had a different cultural experience that
textbooks did not acknowledge or reflect, implying that such books were
biased in how the material was presented. (African American kids were
known to color the faces of people in children's books brown with cray-
ons.) In addition to their content, in other words, the "process" of American
history (and probably all) textbooks was racially skewed toward a white
audience, something that needed to be changed if education was to be
truly inclusive.[40]

Case studies on a local level proved this was not an impossible task.
In Detroit, for example, the city's board of education had recently
decommissioned an American history text being used in junior high
schools because it was so racially objectionable: not only were African
Americans not featured in illustrations but slave owners were presented
as kindly men and Reconstruction explained from a decidedly South-
centric point of view. Its book pulled from the market, the publisher
quickly produced a revised edition that more fairly presented the facts.
Still, too many publishers were simply tacking on some material about
the civil rights movement rather than going to the trouble and expense
of rewriting books. One American history textbook featured a photo of
professional football star running back Jim Brown shaking hands with
President Kennedy in its hastily produced civil rights section, an obvious
shortcut toward appearing more diversified.[41]

Dissatisfied with publishers' efforts to produce more "integrated"
American history textbooks, Detroit became a pioneer in reforming the
ways in which American history was taught in the early 1960s. The city's
school districts had developed and were using a "Negro history supplement" titled *The Struggle for Freedom and Rights* that other districts
around the country were adopting as a model. Also concluding that no
single textbook would or could get it right, New York City's school system
had created its own supplement called *The Negro in American History*, a
booklet that no major publisher dared print because of the fear of

repercussions (especially in the South).[42] Denver was another city in which excellent curriculum materials had been developed, more evidence that the teaching of American history could be reformed on at least on a regional basis.[43]

The most commonly used American history textbooks remained problematic. The presence of free blacks in the antebellum era was difficult at best to find in the books, for example, as was any sense of the trade skills many of them possessed, and too much emphasis was placed on African Americans' role as entertainers rather than scholars or artists.[44] Raymond Pace Alexander, a Philadelphia judge and self-described "devotee of the study of Negro history," had an interesting theory about why American history textbooks tended to ignore or distort the role of African Americans. "If America learned from their school-books of the Negro's remarkable contributions to American *freedom* and *progress* from accurately recorded history books," he wrote, "the American conscience would be stirred and awakened by this powerful moral imperative." Acknowledging that African Americans had over the last two centuries played an integral role in shaping our democracy would effectively force contemporary Americans to afford them full and equal rights—something not everyone was prepared to do. Whether a conscious effort or not, perpetuating African American myths and stereotypes in history textbooks served an active purpose, this thinking went; marginalizing their past was a useful way to marginalize their present and future.[45]

Much of that was about to change, however, as African Americans realized major accomplishments in the civil rights movement and as new racial attitudes sprang out of the counterculture. Publishers of textbooks would soon be effectively forced to do a better job of presenting the estimable role of African Americans over the course of American history, as the kind of products they had been offering were increasingly seen as racially and ethnically biased. In fact, the field as a whole was poised for radical transformation, just as it had been after World War II as a new chapter in the history of the United States began. There were clear signs that the consensus school of American history that had dominated the field during the postwar years was eroding, with something much more incendiary waiting in the wings. Core themes of the American idea and experience—individualism and Manifest Destiny, for example— were being exposed as mythologies that had little basis in fact. American history was on the brink of another rebirth, one that would shatter the complacency of the field and inject a fresh kind of energy into our looking back at the nation's past.

# 3 E Pluribus Confusion

1965–1979

America and its view of the past are now changing so rapidly that few American schoolchildren in the future will share any common attitude toward their country's history.

"E Pluribus Confusion," *Time*, 1979

In 1965, Daniel Boorstin published the second of his sweeping trilogy of American history. Much like his 1958 *The Americans: The Colonial Experience*, his new volume *The Americans: The National Experience* portrayed the United States and its people as comprising a unique and special kind of civilization. Relentlessly inventive and perpetually restless, Americans of the eighteenth and nineteenth centuries were determined to create something new every chance they could, in the process leaving the rot and decay of the Old World far behind. With millions of acres of rich, virgin land, this new breed of people had virtually unlimited resources to make prosperity and abundance for all a reality. Americans were creating a new kind of government as well, its political system designed to help the people realize their grand ambitions rather than serve the interests of a privileged class within an aristocracy or monarchy. All in all, Boorstin's reading of the history of the United States was a sanguine one, filled with reasons for Americans of the mid-1960s to be not just proud of their past but confident and optimistic about where their country was heading.[1]

Boorstin's interpretation of American history, while undeniably brilliant, would soon come to represent a decidedly dated method of reading the nation's past. Boorstin's "cheerful vision" of American history, as John P. Diggins described it in 1971, was emblematic of the "consensus" school that dominated the field after World War II. For Boorstin and others of his ilk, it was American "exceptionalism" that best defined the character of the country and its people; our noble experiment in democracy was the thing that made us different from any other society on earth. Pragmatic, success-driven, and—most important—unified, Americans were seemingly capable of anything if they set their mind to it. This vision of the country's history reflected the buoyancy of the postwar years—our past, present, and future seen through the lens of Henry Luce's imperialistic "American Century."[2]

As President Lyndon Johnson's dreams of a poverty- and racism-free "Great Society" collapsed and the Vietnam War escalated in the mid-1960s, however, it was becoming increasingly clear to a new generation of historians that America's story may not have been as exceptional or cheery as some liked to believe. The history of the United States was filled with tension and violence between groups, making "conflict" a better metadescriptor of our past than "consensus." America was a pluralistic society, not a unified one, this group of historians argued, and a new way of reading our past was needed. Through the late 1960s and 1970s, the conflict school of American history would gain followers who successfully turned the field upside down by challenging all of its major suppositions. By the end of the counterculture era, American history was a much different thing than it was at the beginning; the field experienced a revolution every bit as significant as that of the nation as a whole.

## The New Left

The New Left, as it was called at the time, was chiefly credited (and blamed) for creating and promoting the "conflict" school of American history. Led primarily by young adults with radical political sensibilities, the New Left became a force to reckon with in America in the late 1960s as liberals and some moderates identified with their varied "antiestablishment" causes. With much of New Left activism based on university campuses, it was not surprising that the movement crept into academic disciplines, notably sociology, economics, and political science. By the time of the 1967 "Summer of Love," American history, too, was showing clear signs of New Left political thought as the consensus approach that dominated the field for two decades gradually lost steam. Most postwar historians did not embrace the conflict model of American history that prevailed between the world wars; they rejected the idea that class and region were each a source of major struggle and confrontation between groups with conflicting interests. With the glaring exceptions of slavery and the Civil War, the nation's past was seen as a peaceful period in which many Americans enjoyed material abundance and political liberties—the first time in history such a thing had occurred.[3]

In some ways, then, this new generation of "radical" American historians ironically shared much in common with scholars of the 1920s and 1930s rather than those of the 1940s and 1950s. The consensus-oriented past of the postwar era was just not "usable" enough, New Left historians had determined, meaning something very different had to be constructed. Adopting Charles Beard as their intellectual hero, these historians looked to the common folk versus the elite as the principal definers of the American experience. For almost two centuries, ordinary Americans were faced with the difficult task of competing with a privileged class, in much the same way New Left historians perceived themselves battling a conservative, aristocratic, academic regime. Not coincidentally, the New Left's interpretation of American history could be used for political purposes, furthering a liberal and possibly radical agenda in its quest for sweeping social change.[4]

The New Left's brand of history—which was, for better or worse, commonly referred to as "revisionist"—plainly revealed how our understanding of what took place in the past was fluid and mutable rather than fixed and permanent. Revisionists, usually designated as politically leftist, focused on conflict versus unity and, much to the chagrin of traditionalists, the nation's failures versus its successes. Fittingly, perhaps, revisionists were a diffuse group of scholars and writers with no single, consistent ideological thread binding them together except the mission to question and challenge prevailing views of American history. Collectively, however, the group formed a powerful movement that by 1970 threatened to reinvent American history both in the classroom and in popular culture.[5]

Rejecting the kind of consensus history written by people ranging from Daniel Boorstin to Richard Hofstadter to Henry Nash Smith, revisionists embraced the countercultural spirit of the late 1960s. While the former contrasted American pluralistic democracy to the violence, totalitarianism, and class conflict so prevalent in the Old World, the latter was finding economic divisions to be a persistent (and disturbing) theme in our nation's own history. With a good share of revisionists having had personal experience in the civil rights and antiwar movements, it was not surprising they used a discordant lens to read the American past. The winners may have written the first draft of American history (or had their victories documented by historians), revisionists pointed out, but it was due time that those not part of the ruling elite had their stories told. Recovering those stories might be difficult, but doing do was vital if we wanted a history that reflected the diversity of the American people.[6]

Essays aimed at dismantling the consensus school of American history filled the *American Historical Review* in the late 1960s and 1970s, each in its own way debunking a popular myth about the nation's past. In his "The Egalitarian Myth and the American Social Reality," for example, Edward Pessen demonstrated how we were not a "middle class nation" over the course of the country's first century. Then, as now, wealth was sharply divided along class lines, meaning our devout faith in egalitarianism was built on a shaky if not outright faulty foundation.[7] Similarly, in his "The Founding Fathers and Slavery," William W. Freehling exposed the "happy tale" that the founders of the country were against slavery as a big fraud. The men subscribed to the racist attitudes of the day and profited from their slaves, he and a handful of other scholars showed, proving that they did not truly believe that "all men were created equal."[8] The collective recasting of such classic tropes of the American experience served to shift the tectonic plates of the field, precisely as revisionists intended.

Even Progressive history, which had begun to fall out of favor a few decades earlier, was experiencing somewhat of a revival because it was in some ways revisionist. In 1968, for example, Hofstadter published *The Progressive Historians*, a generally positive study of the work of Frederick Jackson Turner, Charles Beard, and Vernon Louis Parrington.[9] As at the turn of the century, historians perceived that their field could help expose corruption and injustice in the hope that society could somehow benefit. The Vietnam War, civil rights movement, Watergate scandal, economic recession, rise of cultural nationalism, and other events caused many to take a more critical look at the nation's past, present, and future, ultimately resulting in the formation of New Left revisionism. The stories told by revisionist historians called some of the country's foundational myths in question—myths that helped form the basis of American identity. This casting of doubt on the truth of the nation's traditional stories contributed to a prevailing sense of disunity and discord within and even outside of the field of American history.

While clearly not a revisionist, Daniel Boorstin himself embraced a more populist approach to writing American history. His 1973 *The Americans: The Democratic Experience* was the third volume of his trilogy that focused not on important events but instead on the more common sides of uncommon men. Women were conspicuously absent from his books, however, as were minorities and major sites of conflict such as the Vietnam War, the very dimensions of the American experience that the new generation of historians believed needed to be highlighted.[10]

Indeed, women's history had emerged as a dedicated field of inquiry by the mid-1970s, a natural extension of the feminist movement. Women's history courses in college were becoming increasingly popular, raising questions of how they should be taught. Some professors were adapting the "great man" approach to their own fields by telling the stories of women who had achieved important things in business, politics, education, and social work. (Some critics argued that a "great woman" approach to history was similarly inconsistent with the New Left's efforts to view the field "from the bottom up" and that despite their significant achievements, few women a century or two earlier held true power. There was also a significant amount of literature about the suffragists, making it tempting for educators in women's history to focus exclusively on their stories.[11]) The larger point, however, was that women's history was representative of the pluralization of American history in the late 1960s and 1970s. Practitioners of "herstory" were attempting to diversify the field by incorporating women, who had previously remained largely powerless and therefore voiceless, into the nation's story.

In a 1974 essay for *Women's Studies*, Roberta Balstad Miller outlined what she believed to be the best method of teaching and learning women's history. It was not "great" women or feminists who should be the focus of courses in the developing field but instead "those unknown and inarticulate women who lived out their lives within the confines of the feminine stereotypes of the day." This approach, Miller conceded, was significantly more difficult than the other two, as these women's stories were not very well documented; but it was women's roles within family life and at work outside the home that offered students the most revealing and representative insights, making it worth the extra effort to locate such stories. (Nineteenth-century novels were a good place to look.) Notably, such an approach was entirely consistent with the "bottom-up" school of history, locating the field within a broader framework.[12]

Of course, Miller's views did not stop feminist authors from substituting history with "herstory." June Sochen's *Herstory* of 1974 was, as the book's subtitle simply expressed it, "a woman's view of American history." Sochen took an unapologetically feminist approach to studying the nation's past (objectivity in history was "unobtainable and undesirable," she wrote), with people of color also often portrayed as victims of the white, Anglo-Saxon male patriarchy. Two institutions in particular—family and the church—were responsible for subjugating women, although a long line of heroines from Abigail Adams to Billie Jean King were able to achieve great things despite the overt discrimination.[13] Other groups forced to the margins of American history seized the opportunity to now tell their own stories. Jonathan Ned Katz's 1976 *Gay American History*, for example, focused on the role of gay men and lesbians in the United States and, specifically, the homophobia they faced.[14] With the gates of American history now swung wide open, it was open season for virtually any retelling of the nation's past.

## A Credit to His Race

African Americans, more so than any other group, demanded that their story be considered an integral part of the nation's history. African Americans were well aware that because public school textbooks were purchased with taxpayer money, educators would eventually have to respond to calls for a more inclusive American history in the late 1960s. "If Negroes keep on raising hell, their history will not only be correctly portrayed in school textbooks, but school boards will be moved to buy these books and teachers will be moved to teach them," said one attendee of a 1965 conference of textbook publishers. For decades, historians had pled with both publishers and school boards for the role of African Americans to be presented fairly and accurately, but little real progress had been made. Set against the backdrop of the civil rights movement, the decline of Jim Crow, and the aims of LBJ's "Great Society" of the mid-1960s, however, these efforts were reaching a sort of critical mass. In addition, psychologists were now arguing that how the history of a particular group was portrayed played an important role in shaping the relative self-worth of a young member of that group. A positive portrayal could build pride, self-respect, and confidence, some shrinks were saying, while a negative portrayal could do real, long-term psychological damage. White students could be similarly affected by an inaccurate portrayal of African Americans in history books, they added, as racial prejudices were often learned at an early age. "While a little Negro boy is being psychologically emasculated by the history materials in his classroom," wrote William F. Brazziel in the *Negro History Bulletin* in 1965, "the white boy is being turned into a little bigot by the self same material." Research was showing that bigotry was learned at an early age, lending additional support to appeals for textbook reform.[15]

With the education of young people naturally viewed as a big part of America's future, the representation of African Americans in American history textbooks (or lack thereof) was receiving considerable attention in the socially minded, racially charged mid-1960s. We should remember, however, that "correlation"—that is, integration—was the civil rights movement's initial goal. Black nationalists and, later, Native Americans, Latinos, white ethnics, and others rejected integration/assimilation and asserted greater "pride" in their particular racial/ethnic heritage. This signaled the beginning of multiculturalism and initiated a new era of controversy about how to interpret the meaning of the American experience.

Buoyed by this cultural shift, the Student Nonviolent Coordinating Committee published its own interpretation of American history, as did the Black Muslims; each was an attempt to tell the nation's story in a way that did not present whites as superior to blacks. Communities across the country were also calling for less racially sanitized American history textbooks and pushing state governments and school boards to take the matter seriously.[16] American history textbooks were so bad when it came to the presentation of African Americans that in at least one state, California, a law had to be passed to try to remedy the situation. Introduced by Assemblyman Mervyn M. Dymally, the 1965 statute declared that the history of African Americans (and other ethnic groups) had to be part of relevant elementary school courses, and that textbooks used in public high schools had to "correctly portray the role and contribution" of those groups. Books that fell short in that regard would not be sold in California, the bill made clear, a rare case in which a law was passed that dictated the kind of literature that could be purchased (even pornography was protected by the First Amendment, state legislators were determining).[17]

Various groups in other parts of the United States were taking steps to improve the ways in which African Americans were represented within the teaching and learning of American history. The New York City Department of Education was promoting the study of African American history in general, and the school board of Washington DC had put together a syllabus on the subject that could be used in social studies courses. Southern states were not known for being progressive when it came to teaching American history, but Virginia's board of education had approved one of the new textbooks that did justice to the role of African Americans (while denying that there had been a problem). Publishers themselves had been reluctant to make any significant changes due to concerns that racially balanced textbooks would not sell in southern states. States throughout the South were slowly recognizing that changes in curriculum had to be made, however, as more educators and parents voiced their concern over what children were and were not learning about American history, particularly regarding the thorny subject of race.[18]

Specifically what kind of changes should publishers of American history textbooks consider in material relating to African Americans? Mentioning that African Americans played a role in the American Revolution would be a good start, thought Brazziel, director of general education at

Virginia State College, as this was something many students (and adults) simply did not know. More generally, he believed, identifying African Americans as such itself had racial connotations. George Washington certainly was not identified as an "English American," so why did African Americans have to be labeled by their ethnic background? Mentioning that a certain African American was "a credit to his race," as writers of textbooks were apt to do, was also derogatory and patronizing. Whites were never said to be credits to their own race, after all, and the assumption could be made that most African Americans were not credits to their race if a few were singled out as such. As well, reserving the second week of February as Negro History Week as the sole time to discuss African American history, as a good number of teachers did, was a bad practice that would hopefully go away in this new era of race relations in the United States. (That particular week was chosen because Abraham Lincoln's birthday was February 12 and Frederick Douglass's February 14.) Finally, having two curricula—one "urban" and one "suburban"—was misguided, Brazziel felt; such a policy (which some school districts were considering) was only likely to advance segregation rather than end it.[19]

Some students also recognized that they were not being told the truth, the whole truth, and nothing but the truth regarding African Americans in American history. One of them, Stanley Axelrod, a history major at the State University of New York at Albany, related his thoughts on the matter in a 1966 essay in the *Negro History Bulletin*. "Many history textbooks either distort or omit important information on the history and achievement of Negroes," he plainly wrote, noting that education reform dovetailed nicely with African Americans' demand for equal rights. Besides being left out of American history textbooks, African Americans were treated in a condescending and oversimplified manner, Axelrod felt, with a single sentence often summarizing a particular person's lifetime achievements. (Indeed, Joe DiMaggio got more coverage than George Washington Carver in one popular high school textbook, *This Is America's Story*.) African Americans helped discover America, fought bravely in the Revolutionary and Civil Wars, and were elected as politicians, Axelrod reminded readers, with many opportunities for publishers to more fully and fairly mention their accomplishments in textbooks.[20]

The negative ways in which African Americans were portrayed in American history textbooks of the late 1960s could be traced all the way back to the Civil War. Late nineteenth- and early twentieth-century textbooks varied greatly depending on whether the writer was sympathetic to the Union or the Confederate cause; the stories of slavery and Reconstruction could be told much differently. This regional bias had not entirely disappeared by the late 1960s, and there was no doubt that textbook publishers still viewed the northern and southern markets quite differently. In their 1968 analysis of African Americans in U.S. history textbooks used in California, a group of University of California–Berkeley professors were discouraged by what they had found, despite the Dymally statute that had passed a few years earlier. "We are concerned not only because much of the material in these books is bad history," Kenneth M. Stampp and five colleagues wrote in the *Negro History Bulletin*, "but additionally because it is a kind of bad history that reinforces notions among whites of their superiority and among Negroes of their inferiority." African Americans with nonconfrontational views about racial discrimination, such as Booker T. Washington and George Washington Carver, tended to be featured prominently in books, while those promoting some kind of activism, like Frederick Douglass and W. E. B. Du Bois, were not; this was hardly a coincidence.[21]

The biggest problem regarding African Americans in the textbooks used in California classrooms, however, was that they were difficult to find; relatively few blacks populated the books, and matters of race were given little attention. Students could very well conclude that race in America was an example of democracy in action, precisely the opposite of what was true. In general, the rule among publishers seemed to be the less said about the problematic issue of race the better; it was a clear attempt to avoid controversy. The horrors of slavery, the failures of Reconstruction, segregation, and lynchings, and the conflict associated with the civil rights movement all needed to be included in American history textbooks, the group urged California educators, concluding that the role of African Americans in American life was not being taught fully or accurately.[22]

A couple of years later, Mervyn M. Dymally, now a state senator, offered his thoughts on what he called African Americans' "struggle for inclusion" in textbooks used in California. In a speech to the Association for the Study of Negro Life and History, Dymally told his story of how he became a prominent spokesperson for making American history textbooks more inclusive. As a fifth grade teacher in Los Angeles in 1959, Dymally was dismayed to see just two African Americans listed in one of the texts used, *Great Names in American History*. Surely there were more than two African American "great names"—Booker T. Washington and George Washington Carver—in the nation's past, he had thought at the time. Embarking on a career in politics after the Greensboro, North Carolina, sit-ins (the nonviolent protests held in that city in 1960 that began at the lunch counter of a Woolworth's department store), Dymally made textbook reform one of his personal passions, and in 1965 he convinced his colleagues in the state assembly to pass the bill mandating that African Americans be portrayed accurately in books used in California classrooms. One such book, *Land of the Free*, was soon approved, but now in 1970 Dymally felt there was much work still to be done. "It is your challenge to reconstruct the past," he told the group, the full story of the African American experience as yet to be included in American history textbooks.[23]

## An Infusion of "Soul"

While no doubt challenging given that the sensitive issue of race was at the heart of it all, the reconstruction of the American past in history textbooks offered interesting possibilities. Some textbook marketers wisely chose to avoid presenting a single view of American history, turning the controversy taking place in the field into an opportunity of sorts. Just as its title suggested, *The American Past: Conflicting Interpretations of the Great Issues* pitted historians having different takes on an important event of the past against each other. Such an approach brought the key idea that history was not a single "truth" directly into the classroom, and this itself was a valuable lesson.[24]

Some students, not hopeful that any American history textbook or course would or could accurately capture the African American experience, were opting for the increasing number of classes being offered in the new field of black studies. These programs offered African American students not just an education but a greater sense of personal and group identity—that is, black pride. Tired from learning (or teaching) America's white history, African Americans (and a few whites) of the late 1960s and early 1970s looked to black studies as an attractive alternative to what they saw as just another form of oppression. Recognizing that American history needed to be rewritten in a truer and fairer way, some historians thought it would be smart for their own field to trade upon some of the success of black studies programs. One of them, C. Vann Woodward, told his colleagues at an Organization of American Historians conference that American history could use "an infusion of 'soul'"—a refreshing remark in a field not known for its hipness. Woodward saw such a "corrective in line with the tradition of countervailing forces" not unlike the way in which Jewish scholars brought a new kind of thinking to the brand of American history dominated by white Anglo-Saxon Protestants (WASPs). Feminists were infusing their own "correctives" into American history at the same time, of course, transforming the field in a truly revolutionary way.[25]

By 1970, however, American history textbooks had not yet caught up with the massive changes taking place in society as a whole. A recent study completed by the Anti-Defamation League of B'nai B'rith found that American minorities were not represented fully or fairly in social studies textbooks used in junior and senior high schools. Not a single text offered "a reasonably complete and undistorted picture" of African Americans, Jews, and other minorities, according to the study; American history remained largely a WASP affair. The league had undertaken a similar study in 1960 and while some definite improvement had been made over the past decade there was still a long way to go. African Americans were cast as bit players on the national stage; Jews seemed to have existed primarily in ancient times (and, according to some of the books, were responsible for the death of Jesus); and Native Americans, Asian Americans, and Latinos were virtually invisible. Race in general was typically ignored, leaving students with the impression that the color of skin was not a significant issue in the history of the United States. In an attempt to remedy the situation, the National Association for the Advancement of Colored People promptly released what was called "the first multi-racial and ethnic syllabus" of American history designed for use in secondary schools. With *American Majorities and Minorities*, history teachers now had "an entire course in U.S. history that deals adequately and accurately with Indians, Negroes, Puerto Ricans, Mexican-Americans, and other minorities that have helped shape the nation," claimed Roy Wilkins, the executive director of the organization. The syllabus was not an attempt to replace white history with black history or, in his words, to "substitute George Washington Carver for George Washington"; rather, it included the contributions of racial and ethnic minorities, something almost wholly missing from standard curricula in the subject.[26]

Considering how much progress African Americans had made from a legal standpoint over the previous decade or so, their lack of presence in American history textbooks could be seen as rather odd or surprising. No less than three civil rights acts were passed by the U.S. Congress between 1957 and 1964, each in some way an attempt to end the pervasive segregation and institutional discrimination that defined race relations in America. Besides the bill in California, however, no real effort had been made to view educational materials within the context of civil rights. One could reasonably argue that since public school boards routinely used at least some federal funds to purchase textbooks, omitting African American people from those books was a violation of Title VI of the Civil Rights Act of 1964. Not allowing African Americans into textbooks could be seen as "literary redlining"—in other words, a legitimate example of discrimination based on race. Likewise, American history could be viewed as a form of "segregated knowledge" if the stories of white people were kept separate from those of black people. More generally, American history textbooks could play an active role in lessening racism by presenting a more truthful image of African Americans, the educational equivalent perhaps of all the civil rights actions within the legal sphere.[27]

Some scholars were not at all surprised, however, that the nation's educational system marginalized the history of African Americans. "A racist society needs and breeds a racist historiography," argued Herbert Aptheker in 1971, citing work after work by leading historians that omitted, truncated, or distorted the contributions of African Americans to the American experience. "Tokenism" was the operative word when it came to writing about African Americans of the past, he suggested, part of the problem being that authors, editors, and publishers of American history books were almost invariably white. (Such tokenism was, of course, hardly limited to textbooks; it could be said to have been characteristic of many Hollywood movies, including Sidney Poitier's role in *Guess Who's Coming to Dinner*.) Aptheker, who taught at Bryn Mawr College, explained that all this should be expected as the natural result of a caste-like culture. "This . . . could happen only in America, of course, only in a country whose dominant institutions have been driven to the point of lunacy by the fixation known as racism," he wrote; the case of African Americans was too often casually dismissed as "exceptions" or "flaws" in our otherwise noble mission. Aptheker was hopeful, however, that the new generation of African American scholars currently coming out of graduate schools with freshly minted PhDs would bring a different and truer vantage point to American history. "History itself cannot be fully grasped unless it is understood that integral to it has been the history of the Afro-American people," he posited, calling for "a consciously anti-racist historiography."[28]

## A Direct Indictment of Mediocrity

It was not a textbook but, of all things, a television miniseries that would most compellingly expose the nation's history of racism. *Roots*, an eight-part, seven-and-a-half-hour series that aired in January 1977, was based on Alex Haley's novel published the previous year. The novel (subtitled *The Saga of an American Family*) turned the American Dream upside down with its window into African American culture from slavery to the present day. Haley's own story was a fascinating one. After collaborating with Malcolm X on his autobiography, Haley embarked on a genealogical journey, tracing his family's roots to an African ancestor who was sold into slavery. Haley's heavily researched story, embellished to make it a work of fiction for a popular audience, came at the right place and at the right time. "No other novelist or historian has provided such a shattering, human view of slavery," wrote Jason Berry in his review of the novel for *The Nation*, convinced that Haley had captured something important within the mid-1970s zeitgeist. No novel since William Styron's (much criticized) *The Confessions of Nat Turner* (1967) had brought such public attention to the country's shameful legacy of slavery and, arguably, altered American history in the process.[29] The miniseries interpretation of *Roots* became nothing short of a cultural phenomenon, generating extremely high Nielsen ratings. (The finale remains today the third most watched television show of all time in the United States.)

Like *Roots*, some of the more popular movies of the counterculture years were grounded in the conflict or revisionist school of America's history. Historical movies such as *The Good, The Bad, and the Ugly* (1966), *Bonnie and Clyde* (1967), and *Butch Cassidy and the Sundance Kid* (1969) left audiences to decide who were the good guys and who were the bad—quite a different interpretation of the nation's past. Unlike historical films of the postwar years, early 1970s movies such *M\*A\*S\*H* (1970), *Patton* (1970), *The Godfather* (1972), and *The Godfather II* (1974) also depicted America and Americans as morally ambiguous characters, a reflection of the nation's own self-doubts about its ethical foundation. Much of American popular culture appeared to be promoting an ethos of "divided we stand," a reflection of the then current splintering taking place in the country.

Notably, no such ambiguity could be found on television shows of the 1970s that were based in the past, such as *Happy Days, Laverne and Shirley,* and *The Waltons*. These shows, intended for a mainstream audience, were strictly escapist entertainment, an antidote for all the chaos taking place in the real world. Historical fiction such as Gore Vidal's *Burr* and *1876*, E. L. Doctorow's *Ragtime*, Herman Wouk's *The Winds of War* and *War and Remembrance*, James Michener's *Centennial* and *Chesapeake*, and Louis L'Amour's slew of shoot-'em-ups were also designed more to grab a popular audience than to revise American history. Few would have predicted that the play *1776* that premiered on Broadway in 1969 would be such a success; the musical about the signing of the Declaration of Independence ran for a whopping 1,217 performances, quite the amazing thing given that this all happened in the middle of the counterculture era. The musical *Hair* was running on Broadway at the very same time; it was an odd pairing of theatrical entertainment.

While American history held a prominent if complex place in the cultural zeitgeist, there were clear signs that the academic field was in decline, at least in a quantitative sense. Writing for the *American Historical Review* in 1970, C. Vann Woodward described the two decades following World War II as a period of "exceptional felicity" for history as a profession. American history benefited from the rise in status of academia and, especially, the humanities over these years. Additionally, the reigning consensus school of American history "restored confidence in the integrity of the craft," Woodward believed, with more students, more professors, and more classes dedicated to the field on college campuses than before the war. Books about some aspect of American history also sold well in the postwar period as the subject reached a zenith in popularity among general readers.[30]

Now, however, as in American society at large, much of the felicity of the postwar era was rapidly waning. Course enrollments and department majors in American history were down, especially at Ivy League schools that traditionally had churned out the "best and brightest" in the field. High school students found the subject "irrelevant," polls showed, while interest in social studies and current affairs was growing. Rather alarmingly, the only thing preventing American history from disappearing altogether at some schools was the concerted efforts of professors and teachers. Dissension in the ranks was responsible for the drop in the subject's numbers, it could be argued, with the field's increasing fragmentation and discord scaring off some students. Larger forces, however, were perhaps at work; the "seize the day" ethos among young people in the late 1960s and 1970s could have been doing the most serious damage to the history profession; living in the present took priority over studying the past.[31]

In such a climate, it is not surprising that educators of the late 1960s and 1970s began to seriously rethink how classes should be taught. Recent research regarding learning only added to a reevaluation of methods of pedagogy. Specifically, critical thinking was increasingly viewed as superior to memorization, something that had major implications for American history. According to tradition, the subject—arguably, more than any other—relied on the learning of facts; history teachers had to consider alternative approaches. "It may be more meaningful to expose the student to the process of learning and thinking rather than cram him full of the right facts," remarked Joseph H. Koch, a history teacher at San Dieguito Union High School in Cardiff, California, and it was a conclusion others in education were reaching.[32]

To that end, Koch and his colleagues had developed a pilot program in American history that differed from most classes in important ways. First, each student committed to a "contract" that specified the material to be studied so that all parties would know ahead of time what was expected. Notably, selected material was customized based on each student's respective interests and aptitude; the teaching process was individualized via one-on-one and small group instruction by keeping classes small (around twenty students), and this was seen as encouraging greater learning than that of a typical classroom setting. Independence and self-reliance were emphasized throughout, increasingly shifting the responsibility from the teacher to the student. Such an approach could go a long way to revitalizing American history at the high school level, Koch and others believed, the teaching of the subject being more problematic than the subject itself.[33]

The turmoil taking place in the field around 1970 was national in scope, with educators at various levels invested in the subject struggling to find a way to save it from extinction. "American history is coming under attack," wrote Robert L. Dunlap, a teacher at West Senior High School in Aurora, Illinois, that year. Like many high school history teachers across the country, Dunlap was dealing with the "relevancy" problem, finding that his students were just not interested in the subject as it was typically taught. With the field in disarray, its textbooks a source of considerable controversy, and the audience for those books keener on learning about other things, Dunlap had no choice but to abandon taking a traditional approach to teaching the subject. Dunlap and his colleagues had, however, come up with something they felt was more likely to make teenagers excited about what had happened in their country a long (or not so long) time ago. In lieu of a textbook and a lone instructor, a five-person team used a variety of materials to teach the subject through a conceptual framework. In other words, rather than learn dates of important events and the achievements of great (white) men, students became familiar with such key themes of the American experience as mobility, reform, and intolerance. Lectures were kept to a minimum, replaced by seminars that allowed students to more actively participate in class discussions.[34]

Unfortunately the innovative American history program at West Aurora was more the exception than the rule. A study of forty eleventh grade American history classes the following year revealed—as Harry G. Miller, an assistant professor of secondary education at Southern Illinois University, put it—that "in spite of all the innovative stirrings and fanfares, business as usual is being conducted in the classroom." For one thing, American history had often been rebranded as "new social studies," a vague label that placated critics because it suggested that the subject was both broader and more of a science. "Current events" augmented the history portion of classes, this being a way to increase the perceived relevancy of the subject. Textbooks were used in almost all of the classes, with reading assignments a major portion of the workload. Exams were typically objective and factual in nature, employing true-or-false, matching, completion, and multiple-choice questions. Recollection and recitation, rather than critical thinking, was how knowledge was generally measured. Class discussion was of the question-and-answer variety, with students responding to teachers' queries in a parrot-like fashion. Many classes included a period for "study time" during which students could read the textbook or, in some cases, do whatever schoolwork they wanted. "The surprising lack of imagination and independence on the part of American history teachers is certainly a direct indictment of mediocrity," concluded Miller, and it was a fair assessment of the situation.[35]

## Star-Spangled Fun

Fortunately, both teachers and those in the entertainment business had a once-in-a-lifetime opportunity to rouse Americans' interest in their country's past. America's bicentennial in 1976 was an ideal happening to examine and celebrate the nation's history and, perhaps revive citizens' patriotic spirit. With an act of Congress creating the American Revolution Bicentennial Administration, the observance (officially running from March 1, 1975, to December 31, 1976) quickly became an event of keen interest among many Americans in the mid-1970s. (The federal government began thinking about how the event should be commemorated a full decade earlier, when LBJ had established a fifty-member commission.) Some justifiably worried that the historical significance of the two hundredth anniversary of the colonies' declaration of independence would be obscured by the commercial possibilities for marketers eager to cash in on the spectacle surrounding the event. By 1975 the media had certainly caught bicentennial fever, with newspapers, magazines, and television networks all using the event as a platform to catch readers' and viewers' attention. The climax of the bicentennial would no doubt be on July 4, 1976, with an expected flurry of fireworks and speeches perhaps not seen or heard since the nation's centennial a century earlier.

A full two years before that big day, however, television producers were busy creating and airing bicentennial-themed content. NBC had in the works an adaptation of Carl Sandburg's classic biography of Abraham Lincoln, and PBS was putting together a show on the Adamses. CBS was going positively bicentennial happy, producing 732 "Bicentennial Minutes" that started running on July 4, 1974. Each sixty-second segment was a morsel of American history narrated by a notable figure. In one, legendary actor Charlton Heston spoke George Washington's words upon hearing news of the Boston Tea Party, while in another Jean Stapleton (currently playing Edith on the top-rated television show *All in the Family*) read Martha Washington's formula for keeping cherries from spoiling.[36]

The federal government could not itself resist doing some marketing around the bicentennial. New coins were designed and minted for the anniversary and, judging by the number planned to be produced (300 million Eisenhower dollars, 550 million Kennedy half-dollars, and 1.6 billion Washington quarters), were fully intended to be used rather than just become collectors' items. The front sides of the coins remained the same except for a new date ("1776–1976"), while their reverse sides all featured new images (the Liberty Bell and a cratered moon for the dollar; Independence Hall for the half dollar; and a colonial drummer boy for the quarter).[37] The government also issued a number of ten-cent bicentennial stamps in September 1975, some featuring images of key conflicts like the Battles of Bunker Hill, Lexington, and Concord. Unfortunately, the postage rate for a first-class letter had been raised to thirteen cents just three months later, an apt symbol of the raging inflation of the times.

People of all sorts weighed in on the significance of the bicentennial and how the event was as much about the nation's future as its past. Plenty could be learned from a closer familiarity with the circumstances of the American Revolution, some of those with an appreciation for the past advised, with all Americans to gain valuable lessons in the principles of democracy. "What better way to celebrate our two hundredth anniversary than by using part of the time, energy, and money expended for the observance to make a serious study of how the American experience in the era of the Revolution might be applied to the future of mankind?" asked Bruno Bitker, a member of the Wisconsin Bicentennial Observance Commission.[38] With the tragedy of the Vietnam War still fresh in Americans' minds, a refresher in the country's historical role in international relations could be especially helpful. "Perhaps the most valuable lesson which the Bicentennial can impart to foreign policy is that world leadership is not a possession which can be inherited, but a privilege, for which every generation must strive anew," believed Felix Gilbert, a Princeton University professor.[39]

With such an important anniversary looming, "serious" American history was for a relatively brief period of time extremely popular, with sources high and low effectively promoting the event. *Time*, for example, asked leading American historian Daniel J. Boorstin to write a bicentennial essay for the magazine in 1975, giving a very large audience a tutorial in the nation's founding. In his essay (he also served as an adviser to *Time* on the series), Boorstin reminded readers that our nation was a "byproduct"—that the goal of the Revolutionary War was independence rather than nationhood.[40] Other bicentennial essays, which ran through early 1976, focused on the presidency, work, child rearing, science, communications, art, food, health care, and law. *Time*, which was ubiquitous before the advent of cable news in the 1980s, had already had a bicentennial hit with its special "July 4, 1976" issue. The issue (featuring Thomas Jefferson on the cover) was especially popular with schools and organizations, particularly because it could be purchased at bulk rates. The first run of 5.4 million copies nearly sold out in three weeks, compelling the publisher to order a second printing—the first in the magazine's history.[41]

With a general public rather suddenly interested in the nation's past because of the approaching bicentennial, nonprofessional historians could now present themselves and be perceived as experts in the field. Back in 1973, for example, John D. Rockefeller III, the head of the Rockefeller Foundation, offered a history lesson to an audience at the University of Arkansas on the two hundredth anniversary of Parliament's passage of the Tea Act, which subsequently led to the Tea Party and Revolutionary War, something that had major relevance today. The country was now in the early stages of what Rockefeller called "the Second American Revolution," with a number of movements that had surfaced or escalated over the last decade—the counterculture, civil rights, women's liberation, environmentalism, and consumerism movements—all part of this second revolution. Rather than being an economically stagnant, socially traumatic time, Rockefeller proposed, it was an exciting time for Americans. "I see the Second American Revolution as a positive and promising social force," he stated, countering critics who maintained that the country was in decline and had lost its way.[42]

S. I. Hayakawa, working for the administration of President Richard Nixon in 1974, also made the point that things were not as bad as they seemed as the bicentennial neared. Life expectancy was a lot longer than it was at the turn of the twentieth century, for one thing—this despite all the worrying that pollution and pesticides had poisoned the water, air, and land. The "good old days" were not that great, Hayakawa reminded readers of the *Saturday Evening Post,* many of them no doubt nostalgic for a simpler time. Crime, drug addiction, and prostitution were all more prevalent a century earlier, putting the concerns over those very same social ills in historical context. Child labor was common, and there were no government safety nets for those unable to support themselves. Many diseases had been controlled or conquered, and racism, while still a big problem, was not nearly as bad. And while many major cities were currently going through tough times, the urban landscape at the turn of the century had by no means been a paradise: horse dung had littered the streets, and every year thousands of the animals had been abandoned when they dropped dead, thus spawning disease. "I'll take carbon monoxide," Hayakawa remarked, thinking life at the time of America's centennial was considerably worse than at its bicentennial.[43]

Conservatives, in particular, viewed the bicentennial as an ideal opportunity to reflect on the nation's achievements and anticipate what may lie ahead. "This Bicentennial celebration of the birth of the United States of America is more than a parade of our national past," wrote President Gerald Ford in the *Saturday Evening Post*; "it is a preview of our future." The magazine had devoted a special issue to the bicentennial in July–August 1976, and who better than the president of the United States to comment on the two hundredth anniversary of the Declaration of Independence? In addition to the usual flag waving, Ford (or his speechwriter) could not resist doing a little politicking in his brief message. "The independence for which every American yearns . . . is the unfinished business of our Bicentennial," he declared, drawing upon classic Republican ideology as part of his ongoing battle to trim government bureaucracy and spending.[44]

As might be expected, the bicentennial intersected directly with the ongoing debate over how American history should be learned and taught. One of the more interesting collisions occurred between the left-leaning American Library Association (ALA) and the decidedly conservative *National Review*. With the bicentennial right around the corner, the ALA issued a reading list for Americans to use as a resource through which to learn more about their nation's past. Editors of the *National Review* considered the ALA list to be nothing less than a "fiasco," filled with revisionist histories that did an injustice to the country's proud achievements. (Minorities were featured prominently in the list of books, and there was no shortage of critical interpretations of the nation's story.) That the compilation of the ALA list had been partially funded by a grant from the National Endowment for the Humanities was even more concern for alarm to the magazine's editors. In response, the *National Review* published its own list in May 1976, one that its editors believed was "better balanced and much less condescending to its intended audience." Books by authors such as Frederick Lewis Allen, Daniel Boorstin, Shelby Foote,

Walt Whitman, and even Benjamin Franklin and Thomas Jefferson could be found on the magazine's recommended reading list.[45]

With a certain level of pride in the nation restored, it did indeed appear that most Americans preferred the kind of books on the conservative magazine's list. America was a significantly different place in the mid-1970s than it had been just five years earlier, something that could be detected by trends in historical literature. As Michael Kammen noted in the *American Scholar*, American history was decidedly "out" in popular culture as the 1960s ended but had rebounded nicely by 1974. Indeed, the most popular work of fiction that year was Gore Vidal's *Burr*, while in nonfiction it was *Alistair Cooke's America*, each book a celebration of sorts of our national origins. The two hundredth anniversary of the Declaration of Independence was shaping and/or reflecting a return to a more traditional narrative of American history, at least if tastes in popular literature were a fair measure.[46] Authors of children's books also used the bicentennial to offer readers knowledge on the subject; one of them, James Razzi's 1976 *Star-Spangled Fun!*, showed kids and their parents how to construct replicas of such late eighteenth-century artifacts as a quill pen, a New Amsterdam tulip, a candleholder, a flintlock pistol, and wampum.[47] The bicentennial was clearly bringing back some semblance of patriotism to popular culture, and patriotism was something that had been conspicuously absent in the past decade.

When the dust of the bicentennial had settled, however, many Americans could not help but be disappointed by the occasion. Over twelve thousand communities across the country had celebrated the event in some way (tree plantings were especially popular), with a couple of them truly spectacular. The tall ships sailing into New York Harbor became an unforgettable memory for those who had seen the event on television or live, as was the collection of covered wagons that converged at Valley Forge. But even these fell well short of what the bicentennial perhaps could have been—an opportunity to launch much-needed social reforms. All the parades and fireworks were certainly entertaining but, as some reasonably asked, couldn't we have accomplished something more substantive and enduring that would have somehow improved the lives of the American people? Others complained about the $50 million the administration spent on the event, unhappy that their taxes went toward such frivolity during some very tough economic times, even though corporations, other organizations, and state and local governments also picked up some of the tab.[48]

John W. Warner, who had headed up the bicentennial initiative for the Nixon and Ford administrations, dismissed such criticism. "Admittedly, the Bicentennial failed to meet the expectations of some . . . but it rekindled the 'can do' spirit that has been the fiber and strength of this nation," he wrote in 1977, proud of the giant party that had been thrown. Americans had regained some of the swagger that had been lost in the late 1960s and early 1970s, he felt, and the grand celebration of the nation's past was cause to be optimistic about the future. Reeling from the Vietnam War, the Watergate scandal, the energy crisis, and dreaded "stagflation," the country needed a reason to be hopeful, Warner insisted, and the bicentennial proved to be just that. Warner (who had recently married Elizabeth Taylor) had been under secretary and secretary of the navy for five years during the Vietnam War, so he had firsthand knowledge of how divided the country had become. In particular, the bicentennial weekend of July 4 revealed we were still a united people, something that should not be casually shrugged off. "It is my belief that the Bicentennial mark[ed] a major turning point for the United States of America and its people," he declared, noting that the nation had been not just "rediscovered" but "born again."[49]

## No Common History

While Warner was likely correct that the bicentennial helped to revive some of the central themes of the American idea and experience such as our "can do" spirit, textbooks remained a lingering problem. In his 1975 *40 Million Schoolbooks Can't Be Wrong*, for example, L. Ethan Ellis strove to debunk some of the classic myths commonly found in junior high and high school American history textbooks. It was not only the idea of "the savage Indian" that had little basis in fact, Ellis argued, but also the claim that we achieved "peace with honor" in Vietnam. By the mid-1970s, however, the author was for the most part beating a dead horse. Newer American history textbooks had already largely purged the kind of stories Ellis railed against, as educators increasingly chose what they believed was "truth" over presenting the nation in the best light possible.[50]

With American history in such flux, it was not surprising that scholars outside the United States faced considerable difficulty piecing together a consistent narrative. Because it allowed a view of the forest rather than just the trees, common thinking went, an outsiders' perspective was often more insightful than that of an insider. This was clearly not the case in cross-cultural studies of American history in the 1970s, however—at least not in one concerted effort. "American history continues to elude most Europeans and the rest of the world," noted David H. Burton, editor of *American History—British Historians*, a collection of essays that was more of a hodgepodge of impressions than a coherent body of work. Historians across the pond were making some progress in telling the American story, Burton and his contributors believed, but that was more the exception than the rule.[51]

American historians themselves continued to struggle with the mighty task of telling the nation's story in a clear, compelling way that a "minority group" did not find unfair or offensive. Despite the considerable progress made over the previous decade and half, American history textbooks still had a long way to go on a number of fronts. After a thorough review of the most popular books used in schools, Frances FitzGerald concluded that students had yet to be versed in the nation's true diversity. It was true that current textbooks were now heavily populated by people of color and women—a vast improvement over books of the past—but the downside of this attempt of inclusiveness was that the American story was being told in a piecemeal, disjointed fashion. "E pluribus unum" had devolved into "e pluribus confusion," quipped *Time* in its review of FitzGerald's book, and this was a natural result of history by committee.[52] A holistic (and more accurate) depiction of America's inherent and profound multiculturalism would send the message that we "have no common history, no common culture, and no common values," FitzGerald wrote in her 1979 *America Revised*, and that was something simply unacceptable to most educators. Besides this, she added, American history textbooks remained dull and episodic, with a preference for didacticism over ideas or genuine intellectual content.[53]

In his review of FitzGerald's book, William Appleman Williams felt that she was definitely onto something but was missing the larger point. Through the 1950s, he pointed out, the writers of American history textbooks had attempted to "create a culture and an ideology," such an effort intending to establish and advance national identity. But by the mid-1960s, empire building was decidedly out of fashion, leaving textbook writers without a firm foundation. Should it be surprising that American history textbooks were confused and contradictory given the country's muddled foreign relations in the 1970s? Williams thought not, and wished FitzGerald had located her findings within this bigger picture. "The culture is perplexed because for the first time it is facing the necessity of questioning its traditional assumptions, practices and ideology," he wrote in *The Nation*, believing our present lack of direction to have a direct effect on how we interpreted our past.[54]

Of course, some books were better than others, as Martin F. Herz found in his analysis of how the Cold War was presented in the half dozen most popular American history textbooks in the late 1970s (*History of a Free People, Rise of the American Nation, The American Experience, A New History of the United States—An Inquiry Approach, The People Make a Nation,* and *Discovering American History*). Herz determined that *The American Experience* offered students a fair and balanced history of the Cold War, while the same topic was told from just one point of view in *Discovering American History.* What students learned about American history depended heavily on which textbook was selected and, it need be said, how teachers presented the material.[55]

No one, perhaps, knew that better than Mel and Norma Gabler of Longview, Texas. After taking a look at their son's high school history textbook (*Our Nation's Story*) way back in 1961, the Gablers embarked on a mission to directly shape what students would and would not learn about the country's past. Neither of them had graduated from college, but that did not stop them from becoming by the end of the 1970s highly influential people in American education, particularly in their home state. Any publisher wanting to sell its textbook to schools in Texas essentially had to get the Gablers' approval, and many community groups across the country looked to the couple for making their own decisions when considering a book. The Gablers were deeply religious and politically conservative, and it was not surprising that they found most American history textbooks too liberal, unpatriotic, and lacking a moral backbone. School board members and concerned parents took the Gablers' opinions very seriously, however, and this in turn had impact on the kind of textbooks written and published.[56] The controversy over textbooks was just simmering, however, as the battle over American history turned into an all-out war.

# 4   The Fall of the American Adam

1980–1989

> Although many people conceive of history or the past as an unchang-
> ing panorama that is only waiting to have its details filled in, the fact
> is that the past as we have it in our history books is constantly in flux
> as we ask new questions of it and search for aspects of it that were not
> thought of as a part of the past before.
>
> Carl Degler, "Forum: Carl Degler Asks 'Can the American Past Be Put
> Back Together Again?'"

In January 1980, a new book was published that turned the field of American history upside down. Howard Zinn's *A People's History of the United
States* was, as the book's dust jacket made clear, "a surprising new look
at American history," perhaps the most conscious attempt yet to view the
nation's past from the "bottom up." Zinn was not exaggerating in calling
his book "a people's history," telling the story of the discovery of America
from the viewpoint of the Indians, the U.S. Constitution from the perspective of slaves, and the rise of industrialism as perceived by young
women working in textile mills. Similarly, World War I was presented
from the standpoint of socialists, World War II from that of pacifists,
and Franklin Delano Roosevelt's New Deal from that of African Americans in Harlem. Zinn even challenged the almost-taken-for-granted idea
that the United States was a community with a set of common interests,
seeing the country instead as a place of deep social divisions made up of
two basic groups: the oppressors and the oppressed. American history
had been told from the position of the oppressors but, with his book's
attention to the oppressed, a much different story would be told.[1]

Zinn certainly achieved his objective to, without too much exaggeration, reinvent American history. Those with leftish political leanings saw *A People's History of the United States* as a brave attempt to tell the nation's story from the eyes of those who had not enjoyed the privileges of wealth or power. Those leaning anywhere near right, however, viewed the book as grossly pessimistic and an affront to the country's proud past. Among its harshest critics the book was "anti-American," a codified version of the kind of radical and revisionist history that had blossomed in the 1970s. The reaction to Zinn's book would set the tone for the general climate of American history for the remainder of the 1980s. Domestic politics would prove to heavily influence the field, as President Ronald Reagan explicitly appealed to American exceptionalism as an antidote to the perceived social and political ills of the late 1960s and 1970s.

A year after Zinn's book was published, Yale University historian C. Vann Woodward labeled the developing feud in American history as "the fall of the American Adam," an apt description for how traditionalists viewed what was taking place in the field.[2] The lines were drawn in the sand between liberals and conservatives as a new kind of political dynamic entered the equation to make American history a highly contested site and an ideological battleground.

## A History of Oppression

Some historians anticipated that the 1980s would be a turning point in the field. Daniel J. Elazar, a professor at Temple University, believed that moving from the 1970s to the 1980s meant much more than writing a new decade on our checks. For Elazar, the end of the seventies represented the final chapter of the postwar generation and the beginning of a new one. Many others had measured American history in terms of generations, of course, thinking that approximately thirty-year chunks of time were a good way to assess the life of a society. No one knew what was in store for what Elazar considered the second generation of the postmodern era but, given some of the unpleasant events of the 1970s—the Arab oil embargo and subsequent energy crisis, the Watergate scandal and subsequent resignation of a president, and "stagflation"—many were happy to see the decade end.[3] Amitai Etzioni, a professor at Columbia University, was bothered more by all the "romantic nostalgia and retread pop culture" of the 1970s. A loss of optimism, feeling of impotence, and distrust of government had fueled the trend to look back rather than forward, he suggested, hoping the 1980s would not be a hospitable environment for pseudo-1950s entertainment like *American Graffiti*, *Grease*, or *Happy Days*.[4]

Traditional historians were peeved about more serious matters than the inexplicable popularity of Fonzie. Writing in the *New Republic* in 1981, Woodward framed the "inversion" of American history around a shift from "collective innocence" to "collective guilt." A generation earlier, he observed, most historians portrayed the nation's past in warm and friendly terms and as something in which all citizens should take pride; the American experience was, from the Revolution through the Cold War, emblematic of the proverbial "city on a hill." Despite the obvious blemish of slavery and war that divided the country, the United States was a shining example of democracy, self-government, and freedom. Much satisfaction should be taken in our Western expansion, these same historians held, the taking of a large chunk of the continent being instrumental to our emergence as a world power. Woodward astutely noted that the past that American historians of the postwar years described was a reflection of their present. "That was a period of unprecedented American power, wealth, and prestige," he wrote, "a period of Pax Americana in which monopoly or predominant command of the ultimate weapon seemed for a while secure." As "the policeman of the world," the United States of the 1950s served as an ideal model by which to create a "usable past" steeped in leadership abroad and abundance at home.[5]

Embedded within this triumphant narrative, Woodward continued, was the myth of innocence. American history was filled with violence and injustices, yet very little of it could be found in the "warm and friendly" image of the nation's past that leading historians presented in the postwar era. That all began to change in the 1960s, and by the 1980s a pervasive sense of guilt for these sins had replaced the myth of innocence. The "discovery" of the New World became an "invasion," Woodward explained, and the "settlement" of this land became a "conquest." The "empty continent" had become populated by millions of indigenous peoples, many of whom were killed through what could be legitimately called a kind of genocide. When historians finally began to acknowledge crimes of the past in the 1960s and 1970s, they were the fault of individuals or certain groups. Now, however, it was the nation as a whole that was at fault, with this new kind of guilt woven into the American experience itself. "Thus interpreted, American history becomes primarily a history of oppression, and the focus is upon the oppressed," Woodward summed up, the victims being—much more often not—a particular group of "darker people."[6]

That American history was changing, and changing so much and so rapidly, begged the age-old question of how and why the past did not stay constant. If history was "what actually happened," as the nineteenth-century German historian Leopold von Ranke argued, how could American history change even an iota, much less be overhauled, as it now seemed to be? History was really two things, John A. Garraty of Columbia University explained in a 1983 article in *American Heritage*: both "what actually happened" and how events of the past were presented. It was a contradiction, perhaps, but one more easily understood by the fact that no history was or could ever be complete. Which parts of the past one considered thus had much to do with the creation of any particular history, as did which sources were used. In short, history was a highly selective process, making any examination of the past as much of a subjective exercise as an objective one. The civil rights and women's rights movements had deeply affected the selectivity of American history, it could be said—this being a shorthand explanation for why the field was in such a transformative state.[7]

Looking back two decades or so, one could not help but notice the degree to which the writing of American history had changed. Prior to 1960, the idea of a single national past dominated historical discourse; American history was a shared, collective experience. Since then, however, it had gradually become accepted that there were multiple pasts belonging to different groups, each one having its own experience. American history had splintered, allowing "consumers" of the subject to choose which version of the past they preferred. American history had also expanded over this same period of time; the subject had been almost exclusively the province of white, male Protestants, but that all changed with the voluminous telling of histories of other, nonelite groups (notably, women, African Americans, and immigrants). However, while it was important that untold stories be told, little effort had been made to connect the dots—that is, to relate the different pasts to each other. This was a major problem for some American historians. "We have not advanced significantly in our understanding of the interrelations of races, classes and sexes in the formation of American society and culture or in the making of individual lives," wrote New York University professor Thomas Bender in 1985, urging his colleagues to "make history whole again."[8]

City University of New York (CUNY) professor Herbert G. Gutman, writing in *The Nation* in 1981, agreed there was a "missing synthesis" in American history. "Whatever happened to history?" he asked, believing the field was currently as bad off as the state of the nation's economy, politics, and society in general. American history had been drifting aimlessly for a few decades, he felt, and its lack of focus and central themes were now reaching critical mass. Gutman had recently taken part in the panel discussion "Have Writers Discarded History?" at the American Writers Congress; the consensus of the group was that the past had become more "inaccessible" despite the fact that more of it was known. No grand idea had replaced "the old Progressive synthesis," as Gutman referred to the brand of American history forged primarily by Charles and Mary Beard, among others, between the wars. Richard Hofstadter and others had neatly picked it apart in the 1950s, Gutman explained, but now there was a gaping hole in the field: the social history of the 1960s and 1970s was wonderful but segmented, with little attention paid to patterns and context. The net result was a small audience for and interest in American history, explaining why writers were largely ignoring the subject. "A new synthesis is needed," Gutman concluded, "that incorporates and then transcends the new history."[9]

Carl Degler, professor of American history at Stanford University, felt similarly: the civil rights movement was instrumental in expanding the history of African Americans beyond that of slavery in the 1950s and 1960s, and the feminist movement functioned much the same for women's history in the 1970s. A wide variety of groups soon followed, with the histories of Indians, Latinos, the working class, and gay people added to the field. At the same time, subjects that had been for the most part considered within the realm of sociology—family, childhood, sexuality, urbanism, and environmentalism—were now recognized as legitimate aspects of history. Politics had also encroached upon American history, and vice versa; it was a cross-pollination that added depth and texture to our understanding of the nation's past. The net result was the revelation that our history was no less heterogeneous yesterday than it was today, and that the social divisions of race, gender, class, ethnicity, and regionalism had always defined the American experience.[10]

While a more inclusive American history was undeniably a good thing, Degler continued, it had its costs. "The crisis that today confronts American historians [is] to make sense out of [the] national experience," he wrote in *History Today*, believing "a coherent, manageable story" was now an elusive thing in both in textbooks and lectures due to the expansion of the field. With the diversification of the past, American identity had become a much more complex concept, and our history turned into "a series of disparate parts without a unifying structure" or, even worse, a "catalogue." Another major assumption of the field—that all groups had aspired to assimilate into the dominant white, Anglo-Saxon Protestant identity—also had to be discarded within the new paradigm of American history. "Historians of the United States sorely need to put Humpty Dumpty together again," Degler concluded, "for at the moment he is scattered all over the place."[11]

The falling apart of American history went beyond a shift in academic thinking. Signs of what would soon be called the "culture wars" in education could be seen in the mid-1980s, with American history at the center of the politically charged battles. Secretary of Education William Bennett was understandably concerned about students' shallow comprehension of American history, thinking it posed considerable risk to democracy itself. "To be ignorant of history is to be, in a very fundamental way, intellectually defenseless, unable to understand the workings either of our own society or of other societies," he told a group of educators in 1985, taking the opportunity to promote a plan to address the problem. Teaching American history as a separate discipline rather than as part of social studies, setting locally determined standards, and employing qualified instructors were all steps that could raise the grade of the subject, metaphorically speaking. Bennett then went further, expressing his own view of the purpose of history and education in general. The primary role of schools was to impart "social and political values," he explained, with "values" being the operative word. Lest there be any confusion, Bennett made it clear that American history should be a vehicle of patriotism, a body of knowledge that encouraged devotion to the country. The tide was going the other way, however, which was a source of frustration for conservatives like Bennett. "We offer our students the flag but sometimes act toward it as if it were only cloth," he said, blaming "cultural relativism" for students' lack of appreciation for the miracle that was democracy. Treating all cultures as equal—that is, not focusing on American exceptionalism—was where American history had gone astray, Bennett argued; he urged educators to adopt the philosophy that the United States was, in his words, "the last best hope on earth."[12]

## A History Gap

Outside of any political issues, teaching American history at any level could be a frustrating affair in the early 1980s. Lillian Stewart Carl told her sad story to *Smithsonian* in 1982 after recently quitting her job teaching American History 101 at a community college. "Their exams were full of misspellings, misapprehensions, malapropisms and sheer ignorance, no matter how many times I had outlined the relevant points," she recounted, amazed at some of the things that came out of some students' brains. One thought that *Uncle Tom's Cabin* was about a slave who was somehow able to take up digs in a cozy cottage on a plantation, and many were convinced that Pennsylvania had been founded by the "Quackers." "I always had a vision of Donald or Daffy Duck waddling the narrow streets of Philadelphia," Carl quipped. "Gorilla" warfare was commonly fought during the American Revolution, she also reported, and according to one student it was that war that inspired Thomas Paine's *Common Science*. Following three years of this, Carl decided to embark on a new profession that, ironically, had a lot in common with her ex-students' exams: writing fiction.[13]

Happily, teaching American history did not have to make one run for the hills. Teachers at Central High School in Tuscaloosa, Alabama, had a much better experience than did Carl with a new program that took an unorthodox approach to learning history. A 1979 federal ruling forced an exclusively white high school and an exclusively African American high school in the city to merge, ending racial segregation but sparking a host of problems. Many students felt no connection to the newly formed school, something that translated into a lack of participation in extracurricular activities and, worse, not showing up for classes. Recognizing that some kind of action had to be taken, a committee from nearby University of Alabama conceived what it called the American Studies Program as a way to engage the high school students in community life. Meeting in the city's old jail, juniors and seniors were assigned the mission of exploring their common and uncommon heritage by studying the area's rich past and getting involved in local politics. Students attended town meetings and took field trips to historic sites such as a Civil War–era plantation, with seminars rounding out the interactive part of the program. Morale improved immensely due to the innovative program, and bringing history to life offered students a more meaningful experience than that found in a typical classroom setting.[14]

Few schools took such effort to making American history so personally relevant, however. The subject could be said to have been in a regressive mode the previous couple of decades, a trend that showed no sign of reversing. In 1985, Diane Ravitch wrote an article for the *New York Times Magazine* that detailed the degree to which the field had declined over the past generation. The government may not have been banning the teaching of history as a form of mind control—the scenario in Aldous Huxley's *Brave New World*—but there was no doubt that school districts had been squeezing the subject out of high school curricula since the early 1960s. World history had been dropped from most districts, leaving students with just one year of American history. Many European countries required that history be taught every year from seventh through twelfth grades, leaving American students in the dust when it came to knowledge of the past. Was it any wonder that young people were indifferent at best when it came to history, and that many lacked even a basic understanding of the nation's incredible past?[15]

As a historian of education Ravitch was a firm believer in the importance of teaching and learning of history and planned to do something about this sad situation. She was working with the National Assessment of Educational Progress (NAEP) to find out exactly what high school seniors did or didn't know about American history through a nationwide study. From personal experience, she had concluded, it was not much. Ravitch had recently completed a college lecture circuit, in which she visited some thirty campuses. "I was astonished by questions from able students about the most elementary facts of American history," she reported; at a university in Minnesota, for example, none of thirty students she spoke to were the least bit familiar with the Supreme Court's *Brown v. Board of Education* decision of 1954 outlawing racial segregation in public schools. Important characters in American history such as the suffragette Jane Addams or civil rights pioneer W. E. B. Du Bois were nowhere to be found on students' radar, leading Ravitch to start asking college professors about their experience in classrooms. The history professors confirmed Ravitch's worst fears. "My students are not stupid, but they have an abysmal background in American, or any other kind of history," said a professor at one of the CUNY colleges, while another reported that her students "have no historical knowledge on which to draw when they enter college."[16]

From her college tour it was apparent to Ravitch that the real problem was at the high school level. Students were arriving at college essentially historically illiterate, making it impossible for them to make any real progress at a more advanced level. Like a detective trying to solve a crime, Ravitch's next step was to visit high schools to uncover why students were so deficient in American history. Students found history to be irrelevant, she was told by teachers, with no connection recognized between "dead people" and their own daily lives. Teachers had abandoned any kind of traditional approach to history—that is, one in which events were discussed chronologically—for one reliant on "topical issues." It was a nice idea, perhaps, but one that left students with no overarching framework to understand what happened when. In most schools, history had been abandoned altogether, absorbed by social studies. "We don't teach history, because it doesn't help our students pass the New York State Regents' examinations in social studies," one teacher in that state explained. "Social studies" could mean virtually anything, making history a small piece of the pie when it was included in such a course. Some schools and teachers considered social studies to be the social sciences (sociology, psychology, anthropology, and economics), while others considered it to be about social problems (e.g., energy or the environment), and still others about citizenship. Recently, social studies class had become the place to teach the value of cultural diversity, illustrating that the subject could mean pretty much anything except, apparently, American history.[17]

The results of a pilot study conducted by Ravitch and the NAEP were soon in and were not pretty. Two-thirds of the two hundred seventeen-year-olds surveyed could not say during which half-century the Civil War took place, and three-fourths could not identify e. e. cummings, Carl Sandburg, Henry David Thoreau, or Walt Whitman. A third believed that Christopher Columbus made his journey to the New World after 1750, apparently unfamiliar with the children's history-lesson-as-ditty, "In fourteen hundred ninety-two / Columbus sailed the ocean blue." A much larger sample would soon take a similar quiz, but Ravitch was already explaining the reasons for what some in the media referred to as "a history gap." Folding American history into social studies had much to do with it, forcing the subject to compete with geography, government, law, and economics for attention. (Some high school social studies teachers had never taken a single history course in college.) A heavier reliance on textbooks to fill the gap was clearly not working, and the fragmentation of the field into multiple ethnic histories was only making matters worse.[18]

Struggling to find a solution, educators in different parts of the country experimented with novel ways to rescue American history. One school district in Fairfax County, Virginia, adopted what could be considered an arts-based approach, viewing American history through the lens of literature, architecture, fine art, and music. A district in San Juan, California, had had some success with such an interdisciplinary pedagogy that was seemingly inspired by university-level American studies programs. Other school districts were pairing up their teachers with local university professors to improve the former's history "chops." Yet others were deciding that "personalizing" American history was the best way to get students engaged in the subject. Teachers might appear in the form of a real but obscure colonist from the Revolutionary War era, or use actual letters from people of the period to move well beyond the formality and distance of textbooks. Depending on one's view, American history was either in free fall or in a state of exciting reinvention; no one was really able to say which.[19]

A couple years after making public the findings of her pilot study, Ravitch and Chester Finn Jr. published *What Do Our 17-Year-Olds Know?*, a book reporting the results of a history and literature test taken by about 7,800 high school juniors across the country. As with the smaller study, the news was not good. The authors gave the seventeen-year-olds a collective failing grade of 54 in history and 52 in literature after learning that, for example, a full third of the sample did not know that the phrase "life, liberty, and the pursuit of happiness" derived from the Declaration of Independence. Ravitch and Finn concluded that young people were unaware of things of which they should be aware, and worried that the results of the test did not bode well for the future of the nation.[20] Being good citizens and good parents relied on a thorough knowledge of the nation's past, they felt; not being able to maintain our "competitive edge" over other countries because of an inferior education was another major concern.[21]

## A Swiftly Moving Train

If there was any consolation, perhaps, Europeans and Soviets knew even less about the history of the United States than did Americans. A brief comparison of foreigners' understanding (or misunderstanding) of our nation's past to that of Americans' helps put the problems of the field in a broader context and illustrates that significant gaps in historical knowledge were not at all unusual. Most of those across the pond had some familiarity with our Revolutionary and Civil Wars and knew, of course, that we played a key role in the two world wars. If there was any single image of our past, however, it typically had something to do with our Western frontier, an image gained principally through Hollywood films.

Why did Europeans not care very much about American history, except that which could be found in a John Wayne or Clint Eastwood movie? The old chestnut that the United States was a relatively young country and thus did not have much of a history could be partially at blame, as could the belief that Americans themselves did not have much interest in their own past. A more compelling answer to Europeans' indifference to American history was that so much had changed in the world since World War II that anything that happened before it seemed not as important. Quite simply, the Cold War of the 1950s and 1960s, the energy crisis of the 1970s, and the endless economic and political problems of the last few decades were seen as more relevant than anything that took place here in the eighteenth or nineteenth centuries. Europeans, like many Americans, did not appreciate the fact that many current events had strong links to the past, making an understanding of the nation's history a valuable asset in making sense out of the often confusing headlines of the day.[22]

European students were far more literate in American history, however, than the Soviets, if that can be believed. In 1986 Gary Bauer, under secretary of education, examined half a dozen commonly used high school textbooks in Russia to see how the history of the United States was portrayed. Not too surprisingly, given that we were still fighting the Cold War with the superpower, all of them were grossly critical of America's past while conveniently ignoring some of Russia's less than gracious moments (such as Joseph Stalin's starvation of millions to serve the interests of his regime). Russian textbooks ignored our religious freedoms and two-party system while emphasizing our history of violence, poverty, racism, and self-indulgence. Although it would be difficult to overstate our mistreatment of the Indians during the expansion of the West in the nineteenth century, the books did just that by accusing the U.S. military of using "monstrous bacteriological warfare" (smallpox-infested blankets, to be specific) against them. We fought Would War II not to defend democracy, Soviet students learned, but as an opportunity to further our global power by destroying Germany and Japan. Our involvement in the Cuban Missile Crisis was too easy a target to resist, of course, with only the efforts of Soviet leaders saving us from an all-out thermonuclear war.[23]

If Russian textbooks treated our history unfairly, we paid the Soviets back by making them the go-to enemy in our popular culture. In the movies, spy novels, and even advertising of the 1980s, Russians were often the sinister characters, replacing the Nazis and, before that, Chinese and Japanese bad guys. Since the 1950s, in fact, Russians had been cast as our principal adversaries, the opposite of us in every important way. It was thus not surprising that Russians were viewed negatively in American history courses at both the high school and college levels. Even teachers often presented the view that Russians were "commies" who were militaristic, anticapitalism, and anti-God. (Other terms that some high school students came up with to describe Russians or the Soviet Union included "vodka," "programmed," "chess," and "emotionless," David K. Shipler found.) Many students (and adults) did not know that the Soviet Union and the United States were on the same side in World War II, and some thought that the two countries had actually fought against each other. American textbooks minimized the Soviets' role in the war, presenting them almost as bystanders in the conflict. The books also tended to be stuck in Stalin's era, ignoring the fact that much of Soviet life had changed in the last few decades.[24]

Getting Russian history wrong was one of the lesser problems of American history textbooks. Many educators loudly complained about the books in the 1980s, seeing them as a big part of the troubles in the field. Gilbert Sewall was the most vocal of critics, arguing that it should not come as a surprise that students were not attracted to the subject given textbooks' startling lack of literary merit. "Names and episodes dart past like telephone poles seen from the window of a swiftly moving train," he wrote in *Education Digest* in 1988, considering books assigned to fifth, eighth, and eleventh graders (the grades in which American history was typically taught) to be bland, repetitious, fact-filled, and voiceless.[25] Sewall, codirector of the Educational Excellence Network at Columbia University, did not hold back in his assessment of American history textbooks, even writing a book on the subject. All textbooks received a lot of attention—even more than did teachers—because they were physical objects that served as hard evidence for what educators believed students should know about a particular subject. American history textbooks drew an extra amount of attention because they also served as "official chronicles of our nation's past," wrote Sewall, thus explaining why "controversies over content abound."[26]

Sewall delved further into the unique set of issues involved in the publication and selection of American history textbooks. Most authors and publishers in the field tried to be neutral (to a fault) but, unlike in such subjects as math or chemistry, ideology had to enter the equation at some level. Striking a balance between neutrality and interest was proving to be a difficult thing to achieve, especially when American history was being subsumed by social studies. Shifting politics (often varying by region) further complicated things, making content and tone something of a moving target. In place of a strong narrative and voice, publishers had added a laundry list of visual devices to make the books seem more interesting to students. Was American history itself not interesting enough, Sewall asked, our vivid past needing to be jazzed up by colorful graphics, multiple typefaces, and cartoons?[27]

A clear sign that American history textbooks had been sanitized was the almost complete lack of mention of anything having to do with religion. Religion played a central role in the nation's past, of course, but one would not know that from the kind of books students were assigned to read. Religion was a touchy subject and polarizing issue, making state school boards reluctant to approve any textbook that addressed it in any detail. In *Triumph of the American Nation*, a popular textbook published by Harcourt Brace Jovanovich, for example, God and Christianity were almost entirely left out of the story of the Pilgrims, even though religion represented the very heart of the their tale. Houghton Mifflin's *This Is America's Story* was no better, its brief section on the Puritans including lines like, "The churches were unheated and the hard benches were uncomfortable." The Great Awakening of the early eighteenth century was often presented as a political reform movement rather than a massive religious revival, a perfect example of how publishers avoided religion like the proverbial plague. One could also look to how the history of African Americans was getting increasing coverage but the major role of the church within their community was ignored—an obviously intentional omission. It appeared that public school districts had adopted the government's concept of separating church from state, resulting in a God-free interpretation of ethics or morality. Such an approach, often referred to as "secular humanism," had all but squeezed religion out of American history, something critics—especially the devout—objected to.[28]

Barbara Vobejda, a reporter for the *Washington Post*, also weighed in on what she viewed as censorship of religion from American history textbooks. As with the oddly church-free African American community, one would not know that religion played a key role in the civil rights movement from the books used in high school and lower grades. Martin Luther King Jr. was a "Baptist minister," some books mentioned, but a discussion of his deep connections with the church was nowhere to be found. The church was also absent from the abolitionist and temperance movements of the nineteenth century—an equivalent distortion of history. Students were left with the wrong idea that religion and intolerance of it played little or no part in the shaping of the nation, and Vobejda believed this to be a real disservice. Some argued that leaving religion out of American history textbooks was tantamount to leaving out race, something that would be considered anathema. Even Alexis de Tocqueville, a century and a half earlier, had observed the central role of religion in the United States, and he had only a half century of history to reflect on. Like other "unmentionables"—sex and evolution, notably—religion was considered just too controversial to be brought up in textbooks. Religion was at the core of some of the major issues and themes in American history—for example, segregation, abortion, and our work ethic—and this suggested that censoring it in textbooks was one more good example of how the field was failing students rather than vice versa.[29]

## Imprisoned in the Present

Outside of the peculiar universe of textbooks there were some examples of well-told American history. To celebrate their respective fifty-year anniversaries, for example, both *Newsweek* and *Esquire* decided in 1983 to look back at the nation's history over the course of the last half century. *Newsweek* told its ebullient story through the life of one town (Springfield, Ohio), a sociological approach not unlike the kind of field research done by Robert Staughton Lynd and Helen Merrell Lynd in their classic *Middletown*. *Esquire* took a more traditional approach, tracing the social and technological changes in American life from 1933 to 1983. While unapologetically nostalgic and jingoistic ("It was a time of the milkman every morning at the back door and the mailman twice a day at the front," went a line from the *Esquire* article), retrospectives like these helped bring American history to a mass audience, popularizing the field at a time when some popularity certainly could not hurt.[30]

*Newsweek*'s and *Esquire*'s prideful glances back at the nation's past were more the exception than the rule, however. History remained a not especially popular subject in this country, leaving the majority of Americans with a sketchy (at best) understanding of what had taken place here before they were alive. Paul A. Fideler, a professor of history at Lesley College in Cambridge, Massachusetts, made the interesting observation that Americans' recent "future shock" could very well be related to our deficient knowledge of the past. Alvin Toffler's immensely popular notion that dizzying change had led to a case of mass cultural vertigo and widespread anxiety over what might come next was perhaps in part a function of what Fideler called "the absence of a coherent sense of the past." The future and the past were symbiotically related, Fideler suggested, with the two concepts of time sharing a kind of mutually dependent relationship. (The analogy to "future shock" was "history shock," he cleverly proposed.) An unfamiliarity with the events of yesterday was making our concerns about tomorrow that much greater, as we lacked the ability to place the mad rush of society in historical context. There was thus, this theory implied, a hidden cost to the decline of American history, with our collective future suffering as a result of our ignorance of the past.[31]

The fading of American history in the national conversation was not for a lack of trying. Historians had written feverishly over the last couple of decades, exploring thousands of nooks and crannies of the country's past that had previously gone ignored. As well, the history mania surrounding the U.S. bicentennial lingered, with regular folks still keen on digging into the roots of community or family. Despite these positive indicators, "a vital, broadly-gauged public historical awareness has not developed," Fideler believed. "As a society we remain imprisoned in the present to an alarming degree," he wrote for *Change* in 1984, "fenced in by an undecipherable future and a fragmented, inaccessible past." Fideler thought a new approach to American history was needed to reverse this disturbing trend, an approach that offered a fresh perspective on how our central institutions had developed and what they mean. It was not an easy task, he admitted, but worth the effort given the stakes involved.[32]

Elevating American history to a prominent position in everyday life was a tall order given our well-established disdain of looking backward versus forward. A disparaging nickname for the country, the United States of Amnesia, was well deserved, as observer after observer had noted since the days of Tocqueville. A nation built from scratch, a core mythology revolving around the values of innocence and youth, and a deep pride in innovation and experimentation were all key factors in our marginalization of history. Many Americans simply believed the past to be dead and thus worthless, a distraction from the imperatives of the present and plans for the future. Supporters of history argued otherwise, of course, insisting that there was a direct link between ourselves and those who came before us. Times had changed, naturally, but the same basic questions of life were being asked and, hopefully, answered. We had a lot to learn from individuals who had walked in our footsteps, said advocates of history; the past was a precious resource that should be treasured rather than discarded. Finally, history offered the possibility to bridge social divisions by showing how much we shared, our common participation in the "American endeavor" being something that should not be ignored or forgotten.[33]

Bernard A. Weisberger was one of the loudest voices of what he termed the "falling down" of American history. Weisberger blamed professional historians for the sorry situation, not surprised at all that ordinary citizens knew or cared little about their country's heritage. "The remarkable story of the American past is not being handed down in any satisfactory way to our descendants," he wrote in *American Heritage* in 1987, angry that university professors had extracted the "story" from "history." Their favored "mosaic" interpretation of the past left a vacuum in the field, he felt; much worse, it was diminishing our national identity and civic spirit.

"Microhistories" were all the rage at academic conferences, and this was another sore spot for Weisberger. He was convinced that breaking down American history into a million little pieces, with everyone now some kind of specialist, was bad for the field. The fragmentation of the field could be seen in other ways: academics had and wanted little to do with popular historians, and relatively few of them wanted to get anywhere near the mess in the public schools. How did American history get into such a sticky spot?[34]

Weisberger then answered his own very good question. Way back in the 1920s, he explained, there were not many American historians, but they were as highly regarded and respected as any other scholar despite the turmoil taking place in the field. American history remained a relatively small but prestigious field through the 1950s, but things then began to rapidly change. The number of American history PhDs increased significantly between the late 1960s and mid-1970s, in part because of the baby boom. And with the counterculture in full force, American history was exciting to be part of as the old order was replaced by a new one. In the late 1970s, however, enrollment in the liberal arts, including history, plummeted as a result of the shift toward more practical and lucrative fields like business, law, and medicine. History departments slashed course offerings, including large survey classes for freshmen that had laid the foundation for students who would ultimately major in the field. The departments were now a shell of what they had been a generation earlier, with American history in particular lacking an inner core. Things were bad not only for those who wanted to learn the subject but also for those who wanted to teach it. The glut of history professors who had entered the field a decade or two earlier now had tenure, making jobs for new PhDs scarce. At every level of education, history was experiencing tough times in the 1980s, a world apart from the position it had held a half century earlier.[35]

If there was any good news, it was that more American historians were venturing outside the academy to take positions in public (or applied) history. History-oriented jobs in archives, museums, historical associations, and with the government were nothing new, of course, but now this area of the field was more formalized. The National Council on Public

History (NCPH), which had been founded in 1979, held its 1986 meeting jointly with the Organization of American Historians, a clear sign of acceptance and legitimacy. (Working in public history had been considered somewhat of a betrayal to the academy or, in a word, *slumming*.) The NCPH now published its own journal and worked with colleges to train students for jobs in the field. American history could also be easily found in pop culture, with both fictional and nonfictional treatments of the nation's past a visible presence in books, television, and movies. Alice Walker's 1982 novel *The Color Purple* had won both the Pulitzer Prize and the National Book Award for fiction, for example, and Toni Morrison's 1987 *Beloved* also won the Pulitzer Prize in that category. Could the teaching of American history somehow catch up to these fictional fine examples of it?[36]

## Why Study History?

The controversies in the field made it important to occasionally be reminded of the value of learning and teaching history in general. In a 1988 article for the *Atlantic Monthly* titled "Why Study History?," Paul Gagnon replied with one word: "judgment." Almost a century earlier, in fact, the National Education Association's Committee of Ten, a group of educators who recommended that the country's high school curriculum should be standardized, said as much. Studying history prepared young people to have "a salutary influence upon the affairs of his country" because it offered "the invaluable mental power which we call judgment." Much had changed from the late nineteenth century to the late twentieth but, for Gagnon, judgment remained the best reason to learn what had happened in the past. Citizenship was a sort of profession, he believed, making judgment a vital asset for Americans to possess if the country was to prosper.[37]

Others agreed that American history offered a kind of civic education, a good reason alone for why it should be taught in schools. The Bradley Commission on History in Schools, a group of sixteen top historians concerned about the state of the field, suggested that learning history encouraged a sense of "shared humanity" and "otherness." The nation's political history illustrated the formation of our democratic society, the commission explained, providing a tutorial in the precious values of liberty and justice. Textbooks did a poor job in achieving this, the group added; they were not very good at addressing such broad themes or proving any kind of synthesis. The books had too many facts, and not enough ideas and analysis, and appealed to what could be called "the lowest common denominator." Having instructors and graduate students teach large survey courses in American history did not help matters, as part-time and younger historians were typically not equipped with the skills to cover wide sweeps of the field with the insight they deserved.[38]

Gagnon believed another major problem with the teaching of American history was a lack of context. The subject was often taught in a vacuum, with little attention paid to the movements and events that served as the roots of the American idea and experience. The story typically began with Columbus, bypassing everything that came before—which, it hardly needs mentioning, was quite a lot. There was a direct link between America and the ancient world, the Middle Ages, the Renaissance, the Reformation, the English Revolution, and the Enlightenment, Gagnon made clear, and this "backstory" was critical to a fuller understanding of our own history. We liked to think of the United States as a pure invention of the New World, but in fact there were indelible ties to the Old World; a greater familiarity with these ties would go a long way toward making American history a more interesting and more personally relevant subject. Most students had some ancestral connection to the Old World, after all, making the equating of American history to United States history a missed educational opportunity.[39]

There was little doubt that some kind of personal experience made learning history more interesting. It was not unusual to discover that adults who had a true love of American history gained it outside of school altogether; in fact, the subject was entwined with their childhood. "Mine has not been a historical consciousness derived from textbooks and history classes," wrote Connie Quinlivan for *Newsweek* in 1988, her summers while a girl providing her with literally unforgettable experiences. Quinlivan's family never took "vacations," she explained, instead embarking on "expeditions" that offered the much more exciting opportunity to "relive" history. For Quinlivan's father, a congressman from Maryland, it was not enough to simply visit a historic site. Rather, he insisted his family reenact history, whether it be pretending to be Minutemen in Lexington, Massachusetts, or Union soldiers at Antietam. The Quinlivan family walked not just in the footsteps of Meriwether Lewis and William Clark but *as* Lewis and Clark, retracing part of their route in character. Her dad occasionally drove their car at a wagon's pace to get a better sense of the speed (or lack thereof) of pioneers as they headed west. (Let's hope these roads were not well traveled.) Sipping sarsaparilla in a saloon in Dodge City, Kansas, tying imaginary horses to a make-believe hitching post in Virginia City, Montana, and pretending to have a shoot-out in an Old West ghost town were all things the Quinlivan family enjoyed while other kids went to camp or to the beach. Paying tribute to frontier notables like Buffalo Bill Cody, Wyatt Earp, Wild Bill Hickok, and Doc Holliday at their gravesites was a particular favorite of her father's, something Quinlivan found herself doing years later when taking her own family on similar "expeditions."[40]

Not every family could (and probably should) have experienced American history as Quinlivan's did, but there were definitely things teachers could do to make the subject more interesting and relevant to students. Ravitch and Finn had found in their study that high school history classes were typically drab and dreary affairs, filled mostly with a discussion of that day's textbook assignment, test taking, and an occasional movie. Collaborating with other students, using primary materials, writing papers, or addressing the significance of that day's discussion were rare. Recognizing the problem, Samuel S. Wineburg of Stanford University and Suzanne M. Wilson of Michigan State University uncovered exceptional cases of teaching American history to high school students that could serve as lessons for others. Eleven "models of wisdom," as they called them, were identified, two of which were described in *Phi Delta Kappan*, the magazine dedicated to K–12 education.[41]

The first model was "the invisible teacher," in which eleventh grade students led the discussion or, in this case, debate in class. The British government's taxation of the American colonies served as an ideal topic for this model of teaching history, which employed role-playing. One group represented "rebels" and another "loyalists," with yet another group of students serving as "judges." Speakers for the rebels and loyalists each made their case, arguing whether the British had the legitimate authority to tax Americans. Students remained in character the entire time, never acknowledging that they were sixteen-year-olds living in the late twentieth century rather than late eighteenth-century colonists. Attempts were made to imitate the language of the period. Things usually got a bit heated during this exercise (they were, after all, teenagers), requiring a presiding judge to bang his or her gavel to restore order. Until that point, the teacher of the class remained silent, allowing the students to verbally fight it out. (Teachers staged the goings-on, making their contribution larger than it might appear.) The debate revealed many of the key issues that were involved in the actual conflict, and this was the entire point of the innovative teaching approach. After three days of such going back and forth, each side presented closing statements, upon which the team of judges would make its ruling. Via "the invisible teacher" model, students immersed themselves in the primary documents of the era, a much different story from that to be found in the typical high school American history class.[42]

The second "model of wisdom" Wineburg and Wilson described was labeled "the visible teacher." As might be expected, this approach was completely different from the former, with the teacher playing a prominent role in leading the class discussion. "Prominent," in fact, would be an understatement, as teachers employing this model were positively theatrical in their delivery of information to students. Continually interspersing lectures with questions, pausing for related activities and, above all else, an animated style of presentation typified "the visible teacher" model. Suffice to say, capturing the attention of a few dozen teenagers for an hour on such topics as the Intolerable Acts (a number of laws passed by the British in 1774, most of them punitive measures in response to the Boston Tea Party) was no easy task, but "visible teachers" did just that, keeping students on the edge of their seats as if they were watching a horror movie. Teachers who took this approach might very well have become actors had they not heeded the call to education, with classrooms clearly a stage on which to perform. Pushing students to look for values, opinions, and interpretations was key to the success, something not to be found in a class heavily reliant on a textbook. Although obviously different, "the visible teacher" and "the invisible teacher" had more in common than it appeared. "Both teachers see history as a human construction, an enterprise in which people try to solve a puzzle with some of the pieces faded, some distorted beyond recognition, and some lost to the dust of time," Wineburg and Wilson concluded, urging educators to consider using one of the "models of wisdom" they had identified.[43]

Hope for the improvement of American history textbooks was not completely lost, however. Responding to the familiar complaint that such books were utterly bland and superficial, a group of researchers asked a pair of former Time-Life magazine editors to rewrite two passages from popular textbooks to see if students remembered more of the material. The challenge for the editors was to not change the content or add material but to simply make the passages more interesting; it was not a simple assignment. "Before us lay some of the driest prose we ever had the displeasure of reading," said one of them after reading one passage about Korea and the cold war and one about American involvement in Vietnam. After the editors rewrote the passages, the researchers asked some three hundred students to write down what they remembered from each. These results were then compared with a control sample of students' recollections of the original material. The findings? Students recalled about three times as much material in the passages rewritten by the Time-Life editors, offering a couple of valuable lessons to publishers: first, American history textbooks did not have to be as boring as they were, and second, students would apparently benefit from more interestingly written books.[44]

### An Eradication of the American Memory

More interesting books about American history were definitely being published as the 1980s came to a close. Within days after Ronald and Nancy Reagan left the White House, pundits began to write the history of the fortieth president of the United States. Doing so was a dicey endeavor given how much the stock of previous presidents had risen or declined over the years. Years, preferably decades, allowed one to place a leader's performance in perspective, a good example of the mutability of history. Franklin Delano Roosevelt's standing had slipped a little, for example, as conservative critics gradually chipped away at the beloved man's contributions and character. Harry Truman, on the other hand, had gained some ground since leaving office, as had Dwight Eisenhower. John F. Kennedy and Lyndon Johnson appeared to be headed in the other direction, while the jury was still out on Richard Nixon. Notably, the immediate judgment on Reagan was already politically polarized, with liberals seeing him as generally vacant and conservatives viewing him as a fiscally responsible, militarily strong president who had restored America's reputation in the world.[45] More so than any other president, Reagan himself appeared to be making a conscious effort to ensure that history would be kind to him by delivering a number of farewell speeches soon before he left office. The world was a safer place, he told a number of audiences in the last few weeks of his second term, and the country's "soul" had been rediscovered while on his watch.[46]

Reagan also had an appreciation for historical memory in general. In his last, televised speech from the Oval Office, the president warned "of an eradication of . . . the American memory that could result, ultimately, in an erosion of the American spirit." He was referring to the changes going on in the teaching and learning of American history in high schools and universities as ordinary Americans dwelling in the margins of society displaced our "heroic" characters. Conservatives like the president felt our historical memory was being erased, that a kind of lobotomy was taking place within education. "If we forget what we did, we won't know who we are," Reagan said in the same speech, concerned that his brand of patriotism would disappear as left-wing historians rewrote the country's past to fit their ideological agenda.[47]

The president was not altogether incorrect. Over the course of the previous two decades, young historians had ushered in the then groundbreaking method of social history by focusing on the families of "common people" and the role of work in their lives. In the 1980s, however, these same historians added a political dimension to their work by exploring how some Americans of the past expressed activism, especially as directed against powerful corporations and the wealthy (foreshadowing the Occupy movement by a century or two). Notably, demonstrators genuinely felt they were being true to the American spirit by protesting or striking, part of a long history of patriotic dissent and resistance. These historians pointed out that it was not until World War I (during which the "100% Americanism" movement cast political or social unrest as subversive) that being a good citizen did not allow for the challenging of authority. Books such as Sean Wilentz's *Chants Democratic* (1984), Leon Fink's *Workingmen's Democracy* (1989), and Gary Gerstle's *Working-Class Americanism* (1989) all addressed nineteenth-century sites of what could be called patriotic rebellion, as their titles suggested, adding a deeper level to the "new social history."[48]

Happily, what had been the most difficult decade for American history to date ended on a light note. Dave Barry's *Dave Barry Slept Here: A Sort of History of the United States* was revisionism at its best, a send-up of the dates and events that many of us were painfully made to remember as students. "This is history without the dull parts," Barry wrote, bending American and world history as he saw fit (the Fourth of July falling on October 8, for example). The Treaty of Ghent was omitted because it "sounds pretty boring," he told readers, while not just the Ottomans were involved in World War I but also the "Barca-Loungers." "Many women and minorities were also making important contributions," Barry repeated from time to time, obviously poking fun at publishers' current obsession with "representativeness" in real textbooks. As we plunged toward the end of the century, however, American history would not be so funny, as the field entered an even more contentious era.[49]

# 5  We the Peoples

1990–1999

> Historical memory is the key to self-identity, to seeing one's place in
> the stream of time, and one's connectedness with all humankind.
> National History Standards, 1994

In the fall of 1994, a new set of guidelines for teaching American history
was published and released to the public before being put into practice.
The guidelines, called the National History Standards (NHS), were a
response to students' dismal test scores in American history, a situation
anyone following trends in education was disturbed and embarrassed
by. Much controversy surrounded the issuing of the 271-page document
spearheaded by the National Center for History in the Schools at the
University of California–Los Angeles (UCLA), most of it centered around
what was believed to be the authors' overt attempt to "multiculturalize"
American history. Although critics had no shortage of complaints about
the content of the NHS, one term in particular raised serious alarm. "Big
business, heavy industry, and mechanized farming transformed the
American peoples" in the late nineteenth century, part of one of the
standards read, the plural use of the last word not going at all unnoticed.
The term "the American peoples" appeared a number of times in the
document, in fact, something considered quite troublesome among those
subscribing to a more traditional reading of American history. The term
had also shown up in other proposed curricula in recent years.[1]

For historians or laypeople taking it for granted that Americans were
a "people," the news that we were a "peoples" was nothing less than shocking. The Declaration of Independence referred to us as "one people," after

all, and the Constitution's very first words were, "We the People of the United States." When and how did we become a "peoples"? critics asked, not happy to see the nation broken up into parts. The shift from being a nation of individuals to an amalgamation of different subcultures based on ethnicity and race was for conservatives truly revolutionary, and not in a positive sense. Even worse, according to this new history, the American "peoples" were in a constant state of conflict, each group competing with others as it negotiated for greater power. In emphasizing the *pluribus* over the *unum* in the country's unofficial motto, these academics were treading dangerous waters, traditionalists argued, and the United States was well on the way to becoming a significantly less united society. "The multiculturalist agenda is shattering the American identity," John Fonte, a visiting scholar at the American Enterprise Institute, declared in *National Review* in 1996, genuinely worried that the core of the nation would not hold together under a banner of "We the Peoples."[2]

Although it was certainly disquieting to those thinking we were on the verge of breaking up into a million little pieces, the upheaval in American history in the mid-1990s was three decades in the making. As in the 1980s, domestic politics were at work, although those of the 1990s were much different from the Ronald Reagan administration's almost Messianic faith in American exceptionalism. The "multiculturalist agenda" that had been working its way into the field since the mid-1960s was reaching a kind of critical mass, as younger professional historians steered the narrative of American history in a new direction. In retrospect this was hardly a radical development; since the beginning of the twentieth century each generation of American historians had in some way reinvented the field based on the way it viewed the world and the nation's role in it. Never before had there been the kind of "culture wars" that were now in play in the 1990s, however, and it had only been during some major calamity—for example, a war or the Great Depression—that there had been a general sense that our national identity could be in great peril. Fittingly, perhaps, the last decade of the twentieth century proved to be the climax of the troubles that had defined American history for many years, with no clear resolution as we crossed over into the twenty-first.

## A Kind of Social Invention

Meanwhile, the crossing over from the 1980s to the 1990s sparked interest in remembering what life in America was like a century or a half century earlier—quite typical of any turning of a decade. America in 1940 was, according to a 1990 cover story in *U.S. News & World Report*, certainly a simpler, more innocent country, but hardly one without considerable tensions and conflict. The nation was strongly divided by race and class, the article made clear, a much different story than the unity the government had projected at the time our entry into "Europe's war" loomed.[3] That same magazine revisited the December 7, 1941, bombing of Pearl Harbor on its fiftieth anniversary, making the solid case that the event served as "the seeds of today's America." The attack had prompted the entry of the United States into World War II, of course, which provided the impetus for this country to restart its economic engine and assume its leadership position on the global stage. We were still living in the wake of the generation of prosperity that followed the war, this 1991 thesis went, with everything from our youth-driven consumer society, flight to suburbia, and massive federal bureaucracy stemming in some way from the surprise strike by the Japanese.[4]

The fortieth anniversary of the Korean War also stirred up interest in that event in the early 1990s. Much attention had been paid to the Vietnam War in the mid-1980s, when a new generation of American historians approached that painful episode with a fresh set of eyes; but no such consideration had yet to be given the Korean War, despite being, like the Vietnam War, an undeclared, bitterly remembered conflict with many lessons to be learned about American foreign policy and executive powers. (The *M*A*S*H* television series that ran from 1972 to 1983, as well as the 1968 novel and 1970 film on which it was based, were undoubtedly most Americans' primary reference point for the Korean War.) The war in Korea was "the forgotten war," it was legitimately claimed; it had largely been ignored by historians and laypeople alike for reasons that could not really be explained. In an article for *Social Education*, Dan B. Fleming and Burton I. Kaufman reported the results of a survey of a dozen high school textbooks in American history to see the degree to which and how the war was presented. Just three of an average of 875 pages were devoted to the war, they found, with even that material quite superficial. With a half century of reflection, however, the Korean War was beginning to receive the respect it deserved, which was good news especially for those septuagenarians who had bravely fought it.[5]

Thankfully, interest in American history in the early 1990s went well beyond the marking of anniversaries of seminal events. "The public appetite for history seems to grow in direct proportion to the increasing velocity of social and technological change," observed Timothy Jacobson in *History Today* in 1991, noting that historical societies and museums (as well as period romances in novels and movies and on television) had proliferated over the past quarter century. Paradoxically, however, there was a dearth of publications about American history in the United States; the last successful launch of a magazine focusing on history in this country was *American Heritage* in the early 1950s, leaving a gap of four decades. Jacobson felt that it was difficult to present history to a general audience in a way that was both accessible yet serious, and posited that our forward-looking orientation was perhaps at the root of this unfortunate situation. The solution, he believed, was reframing American history from the study of the country's past to the study of how it changed over time. Relating the past to the present was the best way to "sell" history to Americans, in other words; such an approach was likely to make the subject significantly more instructive, relevant, and—above all—interesting.[6]

As the velocity of life in America increased, history also appeared to be speeding up based on how quickly memoirs and biographies were being published. Prior to the 1960s important figures wanting to document their life or career history or that of others would take some time—at least a decade—to reflect before putting pen to paper. In 1991 Meg Greenfield of *Newsweek* proposed that that all changed with the assassination of President John F. Kennedy, when biographers immediately wrote books about the man in order to canonize him. The trend accelerated in the 1980s, Greenfield believed, when former members of President Reagan's cabinet told their stories soon after leaving office. Such books were presented as "history" but, given their freshness, were really not, Greenfield felt. "We produce our so-called history before we have even quite lived it, let alone tried to assemble and understand it," she observed, as writers rushed to be first with their version of the facts and to take advantage of readers' interest in a particular man or woman. Such "instant" histories showed their hastiness for what it was, however—something that became all too evident when revisionists, having had some time to dig deeper, told much different stories. The case of JFK was a perfect example: the man was initially glorified, but two or three decades later was accused of multiple lapses in judgment. Presidents Jimmy Carter and Richard Nixon went through similar reversals as a later generation of historians challenged the first wave of biographies written about the men.[7] The then current wave of memoirs and biographers being rushed out would be challenged by a future generation of historians, it was safe to say, revisionism now a defining element of writing history.

In fact, revisionism was about to define the field as a whole. The year 1991 proved to be a tipping point in the cultural history of American history, as a number of events converged to form what would be the "culture wars." Arguably the most significant event took place in the spring of that year when the Smithsonian Institution's National Museum of American Art launched an exhibition titled *The West as America: Reinterpreting Images of the Frontier, 1820–1920*. Rather than glorify the Western scenes represented in the nineteenth-century paintings consistent with the Manifest Destiny school of history, curators of the exhibit presented them as evidence of white Americans' conquest and exploitation of the frontier and its native people. The romance and adventure strongly linked to Western expansion was curtly dispelled in the exhibition's commentary, replaced by the disastrous effects it had upon the "noble savages" and their land. "Progress" came at a monumental cost, the exhibition made clear, the realities of our settlement of the West a much different story than the one told in popular myths.

*The West as America* set off a firestorm of criticism with its unapologetic myth busting. Although Henry Nash Smith had covered much of the same territory in his classic 1950 work *Virgin Land*, critics were enraged about how the American West was presented in the show. The exhibition represented "art-historical revisionism of the kind that has given rise to the phrase political correctness," wrote Michael Kimmelman of the

*New York Times*, adding that it "preaches to visitors in wall texts laden with forced analyses and inflammatory observations." That the art critic of the *New York Times* was so bothered by the show suggested how upset many were upon seeing how the 164 works by eighty-six artists (including Frederick Remington) were presented. Members of the Senate Appropriations Committee threatened to cut off funding to the institution because of what they saw a leftist political agenda (even though the exhibition had been funded entirely through private sources). Curators responded to such claims by explaining that critics were largely missing the point; the show's main thesis was that artists created imaginary scenes for market purposes—that is, to satisfy the interests of wealthy patrons back east who were most likely to buy the works. For Kimmelman and those of a similar bent, however, it simply appeared that the Smithsonian was in cahoots with a radical and subversive element. "It is the latest example of a reappraisal of the history of the American West, the effects of which have stretched from the classrooms to Hollywood," he scoffed.[8]

Although it was merely an art exhibition, *The West as America* came at a moment when many forces were challenging if not attacking the "consensus" of American history. For example, a 1991 report titled *One Nation, Many Peoples: A Declaration of Cultural Interdependence* and issued by a panel of New York State educators also took a swipe at the traditional canon of American history. The report recommended that the state's social studies curriculum be "broadly revised to place much emphasis on the roles of nonwhite cultures in American life," throwing the gauntlet down in the battle of how American history should be taught to students, asserting that because the parameters of the field had been formed around the turn of the twentieth century the proposed sweeping changes to American history were long overdue. In an 1991 article in *American Heritage*, Bernard A. Weisberger discussed how "the American past . . . was itself a kind of social invention," forged by a group of scholars including Frederick Jackson Turner and Charles Beard. These men "factualized" popular myths of the nation's past in the high school textbooks they authored, laying the foundation of the classic American narrative of colonization, revolution, expansion, division, industrialization and, finally, domination. "This patriotic, progressive saga was intended to make good democratic citizens, and often did," Weisberger observed, and the timing was perfect in helping to assimilate the millions of immigrants arriving on the nation's shores.[9]

Weisberger noted that around the time of World War II, however, what was sometimes referred to as the "progressive historical consensus" began to break down. The nation was effectively forced to acknowledge our diversity against the backdrop of our enemies' fascism and totalitarianism, and a new body of scholarship directly addressing the interests of groups previously left out of the story emerged. Social history of a sort had in fact been around since the early part of the century, but by the late 1960s it carried the message that the consensus was purposely exclusionary. Now, in the early 1990s, some historians were taking their position a step further, demanding that the field reject the consensus entirely and adopt a curriculum focusing on those groups—women, African Americans, Native Americans, and ethnic minorities—that had been ignored and disenfranchised. "The stakes are nothing less than control of the past," Weisberger concluded, not especially optimistic about where the field was headed.[10]

Despite conservatives' claim that the multiculturalization of American history was something new and radical, the United States had of course always been a pluralistic nation. Many of the country's best and brightest had, over the previous two centuries of change, taken special note of our inherent diversity, and this placed contemporary "radical" historians in some pretty good company, including that of Herman Melville, Ralph Waldo Emerson, and even a few of the Founding Fathers. If the nation had always been multicultural, one could reasonably ask, then how could our history not be? Arthur Schlesinger Jr., the eminent historian, reminded readers of that in his 1992 book *The Disuniting of America* at a time when this fiercest struggle in American education continued to intensify. Although a devout liberal, Schlesinger was no fan of the multicultural movement in the field, seeing it as often factually wrong and misguided. Still, the country would withstand the battle taking place in American history as well as the very real melting away of the "melting pot," Schlesinger reassured readers; the disuniting of America was entirely consistent with our pluralistic national identity.[11]

### Affirmative Action History

Schlesinger was not the only one to be sanguine about the state of American history even as turmoil raged all around it. Writing in the *New York Times Book Review* in 1994, Martha Saxton nicely captured how much the field had changed since she was a child, and in a good way. The nation's story had been populated principally by old men wearing dark clothes, she recalled, noting that she had never been able to relate to this set of characters and what they stood for. By the 1980s, however, Saxton was now teaching the subject, and was delighted to have a much bigger set of characters from which to draw. The presence of women and people of color had "altered the discipline forever," she felt, and at the same time had added a more tragic dimension to a story that had been mostly celebratory in nature. "Studying the American past today is a complicated and demanding exercise, but not one that has to bore and alienate students anymore," Saxton wrote, happy to report that meaningful stories were now to be found wherever one looked. Notably, she added, the materials of the field had certainly changed, but its primary goal—an understanding of Americans of the past and the significance of what they had achieved—had not. Teaching the subject was more demanding now because it required actively engaging in moral questions but, given the greater gains to be realized, it was certainly worth the extra effort.[12]

Saxton and other American history teachers were especially glad to now have at their disposal one series of books that embodied the new inclusiveness and candidness of the field: Joy Hakim's *A History of Us*, an eight-volume set for eight-year-olds and up, was getting rave reviews for its ability to flesh out the stories of groups who in years past were literally written off in a single sentence in history textbooks. Dispelling myths firmly engrained in the canon of American history by authors of both nonfiction and fiction was not an easy task, but Hakim was able to do just that without being didactic.[13] Alexander Stille felt the same way in his review of the series in the *New York Review of Books*. While teaching kids at an elementary school in Virginia, Hakim, who had been a journalist, was amazed by how boring American history textbooks were. She decided to do something about it, writing her own book and then "pretesting" it on her students. After making revisions she found that other teachers in her school preferred using her unpublished manuscript to the standard textbooks in the field. After it was published, educators and critics across the political spectrum praised the book that had grown into a series, its superb storytelling setting itself off from all others.[14]

Not the same could be said about Lewis Paul Todd and Merle Eugene Curti's *The American Nation*, however, when the classic high school history textbook was "multiculturalized" in 1994.[15] Controversy surrounded the book from the get-go, with critics including Gilbert Sewall, head of the American Textbook Council. Sewall did not appreciate the new edition's "radical gestures and trendy global 'concerns,'" feeling the book was new social history at its worst. Such opinions ratcheted up the debate centered around the fundamental question regarding history textbooks in the era of "inclusion": How can and should the history of women and people of color be told without completely smashing the nation's dominant narrative? Groups not male or white had obviously been neglected in American history textbooks through most of the twentieth century, fortunate to be recognized even in a marginal sense. The revised edition of *The American Nation* was clearly a dedicated effort to reject that approach and adopt something different, but made some feel that the baby had been thrown out with the bathwater. The country's amazing history had become primarily a story of poverty, prejudice, and exclusion, as the emphasis shifted to the perspective and interests of "hyphenated Americans" (i.e., the adding of one's ethnic background to national identity). Viewing the United States through a gender-, race-, and ethnicity-based lens gave the impression that the country was and had been, first and foremost, balkanized, a debatable proposition. Certain groups—notably, Indians— seemed to be disproportionately represented in the book, an attempt perhaps to make up for omissions of the past. Critics complained that this was "affirmative action history" and that the authors of this and similar textbooks were more interested in the market than in accuracy.[16]

The debate over how American history should be taught in schools had been simmering for some time, but it was the issuing of the NHS that made it boil over. The standards had been financed by the administration of President George H. W. Bush and were developed by a broad constituency of teachers, administrators, academics, parents, and main-stream organizations such as the American Association of School Librarians and the National Education Association. A set of voluntary guidelines for elementary and high school teachers could help make American history the core of the social studies curriculum, educators wisely had concluded, and such guidelines offered what was perhaps the best chance to revitalize the field.[17] Dates, events, and even heroes did not history make, the sound thinking went, with the dryness of the subject showing up in embarrassingly bad test scores. The authors of the NHS put forward the notion that history instead comprised issues and, specifically, how they served as important sites of discord among different groups—a seemingly sensible approach.[18]

When the comprehensive guide to the major themes and concepts of United States was released in the fall of 1994 by the National Center for History in the Schools at UCLA, however, those leaning politically right were absolutely livid. Senator Robert Dole felt historians must be "embarrassed by America" after learning of the document (based on the inaccuracy of his specific charges, it appeared that he did not actually read it), while Lynne Cheney, former head of the National Endowment for the Humanities (NEH), found it "depressing." The NHS immediately became a political football, used by the Right to further a patriotism-based agenda. For Dole the primary task of our educational system was to teach, in his words, "American greatness," making interpretations of history that suggested the nation had at times acted less than nobly unsuitable for students.[19]

The vitriolic response to the NHS from the Republican Party continued through the fall of 1994. Republican presidential candidate Patrick Buchanan called the guidelines "propaganda of an anti-Western ideology" that would "poison" America's children, while Newt Gingrich thought the curricula "went beyond the pale." Not surprisingly, right-wing radio host Rush Limbaugh entered the fray, suggesting that some sort of left-wing conspiracy with an ideological agenda was at work and that the standards should be "flushed down the toilet."[20] Romanticizing "the other" was not only unfair to whites but bad history, conservatives pointed out, just as—or even more—propagandist than the traditional curricula.[21]

John Leo of *U.S. News & World Report* was a particularly outspoken journalist who thought the NHS were, to borrow Henry Ford's idea of history, "bunk." Leo saw a direct connection between the proposed standards and the counterculture, and was of the mind that American history was now being written by "oppression-minded people who trashed the dean's office in the 1960s (or wished they had)." For Leo and others of his ilk, the field had been nothing less than "hijacked," our main story of liberty and equality buried by radicals' obsession with oppression.[22]

Supporters of the document saw things much differently, of course. For them the passage of the NHS virtually ensured that the monopoly that white males had held over American history for more than two hundred years would finally be broken up. The concept of multiculturalism itself was the real threat to the Right, they argued; bringing race, gender, and ethnicity into the equation complicated matters significantly, and necessarily reduced the role that the ruling class had played in the nation's past. Confronting America's failings was admittedly a major problem for conservatives who firmly believed that it was an intimate acquaintance with our successes that would produce good citizens. American history was not the place for critical thinking and alternative interpretations, they essentially held; such an approach would likely do more damage than good.[23]

Indeed, conservatives argued, when it came to providing students with a lesson in civics, the NHS were completely useless. Contemporary society was laden with "bad" (i.e., liberal) influences that could steer young people the wrong way, they believed, so portraying our past negatively only compounded the problem. The net result was that students were left with no moral guidepost (except, perhaps, religion) for them to follow. Our common heritage was a valuable resource through which to instill a sense of pride in children and adolescents, they genuinely felt, making a positive spin on American history nothing less than a patriotic responsibility.[24] Yet supporters of the NHS could not see things more differently. "Historians become notably controversial when they do not perpetuate myths, when they do not transmit the received and conventional wisdom, when they challenge the comforting presence of a stabilized past," explained

Michael Kammen, president of the Organization of American Historians, in that organization's newsletter in 1995, noting that politicians in particular preferred historians to be "conservators rather innovators."[25]

The ruckus taking place within the teaching of American history could not help but go unnoticed by the mainstream media. The field legitimately appeared to be in chaos, with no accord on what should be taught or how. All agreed, however, that getting students interested in what took place in the past was a mighty task, with many seeing history not unlike Latin— that is, a "dead" subject with little or no value in the real world. American history in the classroom had in decades past perhaps included as many myths as facts, but at least there was some kind of narrative, something that could not be said in the mid-1990s. "The American story has been lost in the culture wars churning through America's body politic," a 1995 article in *Newsweek* declared, the potential consequences of such a distressing state of affairs still not quite clear. (The acrimonious row over the *Enola Gay* exhibit at the Smithsonian Institution that same year was emblematic of the decade's culture wars.) The accepted tenet that there was no single history opened up a Pandora's box of issues, including not just what should be included in curricula but what the very role of the field should be. That American history was experiencing yet another identity crisis as an academic subject could have been expected given how, by the late 1980s, it had been gobbled up by its bigger sibling, social studies. The demotion of the field showed up in students' rather remarkable lack of knowledge about the nation's past (two-thirds of high school seniors could not say in which half century the Civil War occurred, a 1987 NEH study found, for example); this was educators' primary motive to try to rectify the situation with a set of national standards.[26]

Under a barrage of criticism from influential politicians, the NHS did not fare well in the U.S. Senate when they were put to a vote. The Senate voted against implementation of the proposed history standards overwhelmingly (99–1), and asked the committee that had produced the guidelines to create a revised version to correct any biases. In the spring of 1996, a second draft was released, and successfully became the curriculum model for public schools in most states. The new standards were less self-consciously multicultural and more cognizant of the power of the individual, making those clinging to our national heritage somewhat happier about what students would be taught.[27] The more conservative still had problems with the basic approach the team at UCLA had taken, however. Conflict was certainly a key theme in American life, they admitted, but they felt that making it the prism through which we should view our history was just wrong. America's main story was one of tension and strife among groups, one would conclude from reading the document, a position that conservatives believed was highly debatable. Likewise, why did race and gender have to be the means by which to approach nearly every topic mentioned? As in the first draft, "presentism" pervaded the second, they also insisted, with events of the past too often judged from today's set of values. Traditionalists concluded that for the average student, American history would be seen—to use the language of the day—as a "major bummer"; our nation's story would be one of constant oppression and rampant inequity. "The United States is not a paragon of virtue, but it has much to be proud of in its past," Herbert London of New York University declared after reviewing the "new and improved" second edition of the NHS, convinced that our history was still out of whack.[28]

### The Thread of the American Narrative

It is easy to see why people of all political leanings were in favor of some kind of national standards for American history. Educators in the mid-1990s were happy to see that national math and science scores were up, as were SAT results, but were dismayed after reviewing the results of the 1995 National Assessment of Educational Progress history exam. Just four of ten high school students had a basic understanding of American history, the test revealed, and this after almost a decade of tougher requirements. The news was no better for younger students; most fourth graders, for example, had no idea why the Pilgrims had fled to the New World. "It's clear, as the song says, students don't know much about history," grumbled Education Secretary Richard Riley, sorry to report that test scores for that subject were moving backward while all others (save geography) appeared to be moving forward. (In 1990, Kenneth C. Davis had published a book called *Don't Know Much about History*, the title lifted from Sam Cooke's "Wonderful World." The book, designed to make history fun for students, spent thirty-five consecutive weeks on the *New York Times* bestseller list and sold almost 1.5 million copies, leading to a "Don't Know Much about . . ." franchise.) If fundamental knowledge of American history was lacking among students, advanced knowledge— an understanding of not just key facts but an ability to assess historical trends and explain their significance—was extremely rare. Just 1 percent of the 22,500 students who took the test could do the latter, a sad commentary on schools' performance when it came to teaching history. A set of national curriculum standards for the subject like those proposed the previous year were clearly needed, but the recent "culture wars" made the implementation of such standards a difficult if not impossible endeavor.[29]

Locating the dilemma in America history within a larger cultural framework helped to put things in perspective. While all would probably agree that education in all its forms was a good thing, one had to ask if young peoples' historical illiteracy was really a major problem. The country as a whole seemed to be doing quite well at the end of the twentieth century and was as prosperous as ever, meaning the decline of American history in the education system was not the end of civilization as we knew it. Or was it? Lewis Lapham, the editor of *Harper's*, agreed with the conservative viewpoint that the deterioration of the subject could very well lead to a serious erosion in national identity. "The schools have lost the thread of the American narrative, and without that narrative the country cannot long sustain the appearance, much less the substance, of democratic self-government," he wrote in 1996, adding, "we have no other way of knowing ourselves." Because the United States was, unlike any other country, an "idea," Americans had to remain passionate about their own history for the country to continue to exist in its present form. Perpetuating our treasured values of liberty, equality, and freedom relied on an awareness of how they were manifested in the past, he firmly believed, or we would simply forget who we were and what we stood for.[30]

David B. Danbom, a professor of history at North Dakota State University, also argued that history was important if not essential, especially for Americans. Writing for USA *Today Magazine*, Danbom reminded readers that memory was the primary element of identity—that is, that our personalities were heavily shaped by our experiences. This was not only true on an individual level but also on a societal level, he suggested. "History is society's memory," he stated, with our collective past telling us who we were. History had, of course, played a vital role in creating and maintaining our social identity. The Founding Fathers were captivated by ancient Greece and Rome when conceiving the republican experiment, using those societies' political frameworks to forge our own. In addition, our own history served as a powerful instrument of assimilation for the massive waves of immigrants in the nineteenth and early twentieth centuries, another prime example of how memory functioned as a "usable past." American history had changed radically over the past half century as the field opened up to the politics of race, gender, and class, but even this could be seen as a lesson in democracy.[31]

For those able to think out of the box, taking American history out of the classroom altogether was viewed as the best way to teach the subject to otherwise indifferent young people. Historian Douglas Brinkley did just that after concluding a much different approach was needed to get college students to understand and appreciate the nation's past. Every summer as a child, Brinkley and his family hit the road for eight weeks to learn about the country's heritage, something that laid the foundation for his lifelong love of history. The Brinkleys traveled to Civil War battle fields, historic homes and cemeteries, and anywhere else a good story from the past could be found. When it came time for him to conceive an American history course to teach at Hofstra University in the early 1990s, Brinkley's instincts were to go back to how he learned the subject in his youth. Soon Brinkley and twenty handpicked students were crisscrossing the country on the Majic Bus, visiting the Ebenezer Baptist Church in Atlanta for a firsthand lesson in the civil rights movement, attending a cedar-burning ceremony at the Medicine Wheel in Kansas to immerse themselves in Native American culture, and taking a steamboat ride down the Mississippi River to experience delta life. Readings and guest lectures supplemented the "American Odyssey" annual course, or what Brinkley referred to as a "3-D American Studies course on wheels."[32]

Brinkley would likely have slammed the brakes on the Majic Bus if it was headed anywhere near Disney's America, a new theme park that the giant entertainment company was seeking to develop in the Washington

DC metropolitan area. The details were being kept secret in its planning stages in the mid-1990s, but it was known that the proposed theme park would offer "exciting reenactments of critical times and places in American history," a historicized Epcot theme park, perhaps. (It was later revealed that the park would have nine thematic areas: a Civil War–era village; a Civil War fort; a re-creation of a Native American village; a replica of the main building at Ellis Island; a circa 1930s state fair; a re-creation of a family farm; a tribute to American presidents; a faux factory town; and an airfield featuring World War I and World War II–era planes.) Local residents objected to having such a thing in their backyard, however, so Disney's America (which was Disney CEO Michael Eisner's pet project) never happened. (That the chosen site was near the very real Civil War battlefield at Manassas, Virginia, was actually the biggest stumbling block. Many historic preservationists, Civil War enthusiasts, and professional historians joined locals to push back the concept.) Notably, officials at the Smithsonian Institution were entirely in favor of the project, seeing it as a wonderful opportunity to attract more tourists with an interest in American history to the DC area. Rather than view it as an inferior simulation of history or competitive threat, Robert Adams, secretary of the Smithsonian at the time, welcomed a Disneyized interpretation of American history. "Seeing many perspectives of history turns our forebears into real people and sheds light on our diverse past," he stated, considering the park "a welcome addition to the list of attractions that bring enormous numbers of visitors to our national capital."[33]

Not everyone, however, was as happy to see Disney become perhaps the biggest purveyor of American history in the land. The company had just released *Pocahontas*, after all, and the animated film was not exactly what one would call historically precise. (Pocahontas was a Native American who became an ally to early English colonists in Virginia around 1600; the Disney film focused on a romantic relationship between her and Jamestown founder John Smith, a relationship that has no basis in fact.) Should certain historical events—the Civil War and Great Depression, for example—be presented as "fun and exciting for the whole family," as Disney promised in its promotional material for the theme park? Pundits inside the DC Beltway joked about possible other attractions Disney might want to include, such as Watergateland (in which an animatronic President Nixon would resign over and over) and a virtual reality arcade offering visitors the nearly lifelike experience of taking a nap with President Reagan or having sex with President Kennedy.[34]

It was easy to see why some were skeptical that Disney's America, which was scheduled to open in 1998, would not be entirely historically accurate. Disney had a long history perpetuating classic myths from the nation's past, of course, with its sole mission being one of entertainment rather than education. In 1955, for example, Disney presented Frontierland at its new Disneyland theme park, which—as Jon Wiener of the *Nation* pointed out—featured vignettes of ferocious "redskins" attacking innocent pioneers. Indians were always the aggressors in Frontierland, and the white settlers always portrayed as the victims of their savagery. Frontierland also included, somewhat oddly, Aunt Jemima's Pancake House, where an African American woman portraying the character stood in front of the restaurant signing autographs for the entire day. (No explanation was offered as to how or why the queen of pancakes from the South ended up in the western United States in the nineteenth century. Her fictionality, as well as her racist depiction, were even more problematic.) "Much of history isn't all that amusing," Wiener noted, expressing concern about Disney's or any other marketers' appropriation of the past simply to offer consumers spectacle.[35]

Disney's proposed theme park stood as evidence that, regardless of the mess in the educational arena, American history was positively flourishing in popular culture through the 1990s. Interest in the Civil War and Reconstruction was especially high, with many keen on visiting key battle sites as a new kind of tourism. In 1990 PBS's *The Civil War* had much to do with that, with both the documentary by Ken Burns and the companion book by Geoffrey Ward with Ric and Ken Burns becoming big hits (the film was the most watched program ever to air on PBS). *Glory*, also from 1990, was the first feature film to depict the role of African American soldiers in the Civil War, adding to the current fascination with that terrible conflict. Other films of the decade visited key moments of the nation's past to enjoy phenomenal commercial success if not critical acclaim. *Forrest Gump* (1994) was a happy-go-lucky mishmash of

American history, while *Titanic* (1997) took the historical epic to a whole new level (and remained the highest-grossing film of all time for twelve years). Steven Spielberg revived interest in the horrors of World War II in his *Schindler's List* (1993) and *Saving Private Ryan* (1998), the latter nicely complementing Tom Brokaw's more feel-good best seller of the same year, *The Greatest Generation*. (Spielberg's 1997 film *Amistad* was frequently shown in classrooms as an engaging way to tell the story of slavery in America.) And with her 1995 *No Ordinary Time*, a biography of Franklin and Eleanor Roosevelt, Doris Kearns Goodwin established herself as the go-to person for all things presidential (succeeding the popular historian Stephen Ambrose). Historical novels loosely based on real events and people were also selling well in the 1990s, proof that truth was less important than a good story when it came to literary entertainment.

Given the popularity of American history, it can easily be seen why the secretary of the Smithsonian Institution would like to see more of it even if it was from the people who had turned Abraham Lincoln into a robot. "It is depressingly clear that we Americans are largely ignorant of our history, and with the persistent crisis in our schools, we are becoming more so," Adams wrote in in 1994. As perhaps the biggest player in the "history business," the Smithsonian naturally had a vested interest in the degree to which Americans had an appreciation for their own past. With its immense collection of artifacts, especially those at the National Museum of American History, the institution had a unique opportunity to engage individuals in the nation's history by putting them in direct contact with yesterday. Any particular object a visitor encountered there could serve as the impetus to explore the subject further, the beginning of what would hopefully be an enduring interest in at least some aspect of American history. A better understanding of the past would lead to a better understanding of the present, Adams wisely understood, and this was seen as the real contribution the institution could make to society.[36]

Within a few months, however, Adams was out as secretary (in part because of his involvement with the *West as America* exhibition) and was replaced by Ira Heyman. Heyman was fortunate to be head of the institution during its 150th anniversary in 1996, an opportunity to showcase what was fondly referred to as "America's Attic." To commemorate its first century and a half, the institution launched a traveling exhibition titled *America's Smithsonian* that went to Houston, New York, and Providence in 1996 and six more cities the following year. The exhibition was, at the same time, an effort to make it clearer that it was the public who "owned" the institution and a way to make its collection more accessible to people around the country. Nearly 300 artifacts (of the 140 million in the Smithsonian's collection) made up the exhibition, which was itself so large (50,000 square feet) that it required the cavernous space of a convention or civic center to hold it.[37]

Not surprisingly, *America's Smithsonian* (which was free to visitors) featured many of the institution's "greatest hits," including an Apollo space capsule, George Washington's sword, Amelia Earhart's flight suit, the ruby slippers from *The Wizard of Oz*, a Wright brothers plane, a Tiffany lamp, and a Frank Lloyd Wright chair. Inventions such as a Thomas Edison light bulb, Samuel Morse telegraph, and Alexander Graham Bell telephone were also there to see, as were iconic items from popular culture and sports including Kermit the Frog, Muhammad Ali's boxing gloves, and Dizzy Gillespie's trumpet.[38] Scholars from the Smithsonian accompanied the exhibit to each city, giving lectures and going into local communities to further reach out to ordinary folks.[39] "You don't always know specifically whose life is touched or which young scholar-to-be is influenced by the exposure to new ideas and career choices," said Heyman of the outreach program, "but you know that it happens."[40]

## Radical Gestures

One had to wonder what treasures the Smithsonian Institution would collect and display if it had been founded in 1996 rather than 1846. With American history now well on the way to being seen as the study of social classes and ethnic groups, virtually anything associated with "the great man theory" would have little place in an institution devoted to preserving important artifacts. Rather than the exceptional, it would focus on ordinary people, specifically the working class, and those relegated to the margins of society. For those believing that "the great man theory" still had value, however, American history had been socialized and feminized, but there was still a lot of good to be gained by old-fashioned hero worship (of white males). It was understandable how American history could and perhaps should be expanded to pay more attention to nonwhites, traditionalists conceded, but now some sections of many textbooks in the field had more content devoted to African Americans and native populations than those of European descent. It was clear that the passage of the NHS had had a major effect on what was or wasn't deemed American history, greatly reducing the importance of what had been the centerpiece of the field—the Western Enlightenment. As an advanced version of the "new social history" that had gained ground in the 1970s, the NHS all but wiped out the top-down view of the nation's past for one that was bottom-up. Notably, the American Revolution was now less about the Founding Fathers and more about how the event transformed the lives of the common people. The field's textbooks also tended to zero in on the contradiction between the Founding Fathers' vision of equality and the practice of slavery, with this alone battering if not shattering a traditional narrative of history starring a group of exceptional men.[41]

As conservatives claimed, however, textbook publishers did appear to be reconstructing history principally for marketing purposes. California, Florida, and Texas were the largest markets for textbooks in the United States, and each of these states had a large Latino population. (Recent immigration can be seen as having had a huge effect on not just history curricula and textbooks but also student bodies and the very complexion of American society.) Was it a coincidence that Latinos of the past had begun to play a feature role in new American history textbooks? Alexander Stille certainly did not think so after reviewing a few such books. "The American history taught in schools has been rewritten and transformed in recent decades by a handful of large publishers who are much concerned to meet the demands of both the multicultural left and the conservative religious right," he wrote, noting that millions of dollars were at stake when making editorial decisions. (To be clear, publishers incorporated Latino voices not merely to sell textbooks but to recognize the important contributions made by such figures as Cesar Chavez.) Any content perceived as possibly anti-Christian was carefully screened from American history books, including certain words (*imagine* because it was deemed linguistically too close to *magic*) and events (notably, Halloween). In order not to alienate the conservative bloc, other no-no's included criticizing the country's traditional heroes, describing the horrors of slavery in too much detail, and lauding FDR's New Deal. It had been the policy for American history textbooks to be reviewed by one scholar prior to publication, but now the books were often vetted by a number of academics representing different points of view. At one leading publisher, no less than half a dozen perspectives—African American, Asian American, Christian fundamentalist, feminist, Islamic, and Native American—were sought before a book went to press; the end result was something that was wholly inoffensive and, more often than not, utterly bland.[42]

In addition to how much money could be made, the culture wars, or what was now often referred to as "identity politics," continued to be a major factor in deciding which U.S. history textbooks should be used in classrooms at the end of the 1990s. A variety of coalitions—ethnic- and race-based pressure groups, gender activists, and various religious organizations—were determined to make their voices heard when it came to the books' content. How much and how their groups were presented was a key concern, making the adoption of any history textbook a contentious affair. This, and the fact that the political dynamics varied so much from state to state, made the job that much more difficult for publishers. "Publishers are no longer confident about how to represent the nation, its civic ideals, or the world," noted *Current* in 1999, with the history battles of the 1990s making decisions regarding content very difficult. "Multiculturalism," "world cultures," and "inclusiveness" remained hot buttons in history and in social studies as a whole, but how to reflect those themes in stories from the past was up for grabs. Traditional textbooks like Daniel Boorstin's *History of the United States* were becoming increasingly hard to find in classrooms as multiculturalism ruled the day. Meanwhile, critics continued to label culturally diverse perspectives of history as "politically correct" and argued that such an approach was "dumbing down" the field (and, presumably, students).[43]

Those on the extreme end of the political spectrum went even further in criticizing academics and others who fully embraced "politically correct" readings of American history. Rather than being revisionists or deconstructionists, these scholars were "masochists," suggested Gerald F. Kreyche, emeritus professor of philosophy at DePaul University; they were people who hated both themselves and the United States. Feeling guilty about and apologizing for America's past sins was absurd, Kreyche felt, thinking it unfair to judge yesterday's events through a rearview mirror. (President Bill Clinton had recently apologized in Africa for the historical practice of slavery in the United States, sparking the debate about expressing regret for sins of the past.) After reading some of the more popular American history books, Kreyche noted that it appeared that minorities could do no wrong and white men no good. (Patricia Limerick's *Legacy of Conquest*, about the settling of the West, was a particular target.) Even Ken Burns, the popular filmmaker, was guilty of white bashing for casting the acquisition of what was Spanish and Mexican territory as a bad thing in one of the episodes of his documentary *The Civil War*. "Ask the people of Texas, Arizona, New Mexico, and California if they would prefer to be under Mexican rule today," Kreyche wrote, his logic somewhat puzzling but his point no doubt made. The United States was, comparatively speaking, a very tolerant, generous, and welcoming nation, he countered, a much different story than "negativists" preferred to believe.[44]

Regardless of the approach being taken, the new history textbooks being published were arguably already "dumber" in that they had much less text and many more illustrations than those of the past. It was considered common wisdom that students had short attention spans, did not particularly like reading, or were barely literate, leading publishers to fill their books with graphics, maps, charts, diagrams, timelines, and pictures. This was justified by the theory that a picture was worth a thousand words, as the saying went, meaning students could absorb a lot of information quickly through visuals rather than text. Publishers of educational materials agreed that snappy, colorful, eye-catching graphics were the best way to communicate with the MTV and video game generation. A narrative or storytelling—the way history had generally been taught for decades, if not centuries—was less important than keeping students visually engaged. As well, textbooks were now often just one piece of a multimedia system, with complementary CD-ROMs being part of the package. Although publishers probably would not want to admit it, the "sexing up" of textbooks was an effort to make history—and education in general—more entertaining, a disturbing trend to those who believed in the power of simple words versus bells and whistles. For others, however, anything that could make history textbooks more interesting was a good idea given the undeniable fact that students found them as boring as could be.[45]

## A Present-Tense Culture

The fight over what kind of textbooks to use in classrooms was simply a reflection of the larger issue facing American history at the end of the twentieth century. Two factions, each genuinely committed to what it believed was in the best interests of young people and the future of the nation, had very different views regarding the purpose of teaching American history. One faction saw American history as a wonderful opportunity to demonstrate the nation at its best, inscribing the values of patriotism and heroism in children and teens through lessons of the past. Via stories steeped in success and victory, this group maintained, students would gain a real sense of idealism, something that would serve them and the country as a whole well in the years ahead. Another faction, however, could not see things more differently. This group believed that examining the injustices and hypocrisy of those in power offered the most important and valuable insights related to our past. It was, in essence, our failures that served as the best window into American history, members of this group contended, with such a perspective being the only way to get a true sense of the nation's ideals and how it had not lived up to them. In other words, it was not democracy itself but the big gap between our philosophy and practice of democracy that shed the most light on who we were and are as a people.[46]

Doing yeoman's duty, the *American Scholar* asked some of the country's leading historians to weigh in on what version of American history they believed young people should learn. One of them, William Cronon, a professor at the University of Wisconsin and author of the terrific *Changes in the Land*, could not help but observe how what had been in the 1980s the primary concern in the field—students' shocking lack of knowledge of American history—had been obscured by the politics surrounding the NHS. Cronon was also struck by how ambitious the standards were, not believing for a second that, regardless of the ideological debate, most high school seniors would ever be conversant in such NHS subject matters as the Whiskey Rebellion, the nullification crisis, or the commerce clause of the U.S. Constitution. He recognized there was a deeper problem with teaching American history that was unfortunately going largely ignored in the overarching dispute. "The past is not a living reality for most American children, any more than it is for many American adults," he pointed out, implying that the subject itself is irrelevant without some kind of personal encounter. Making the past matter should be educators' first task, he reminded us, and his own teaching experience providing him with a rather simple approach: "Whatever works."[47]

Christopher Hitchens, the outspoken journalist and author, also believed American's problem with their own history ran deeper than how it was presented. "We dwell in a present-tense culture," he wrote in *Harper's*, noting that no approach to teaching the subject would dramatically improve the situation. There was certainly no shortage of American history on television, Hitchens admitted, with a number of quite popular history and biography shows on PBS, A&E, and the History Channel. Hollywood was also successfully using American history as entertainment fodder, as it always had done, producing blockbusters about everything from World War II to the assassination of JFK to the Watergate scandal. American history could also be easily found throughout the nation's civic arena. Memorials of a notable dead American—typically a statue or plaque—continued to be put up in cities large and small, and schools, airports, and other public buildings were still being named to preserve in memory such people. The ubiquity of American history in popular culture and public life belied citizens' lack of actual knowledge of the subject, however—especially among young people. Even worse, many if not most students simply did not care about their country's history, Hitchens noted, as they found it irrelevant in everyday life. Going further, he suggested that there might even be an inherent cultural bias toward spending a lot of time thinking about the past, such a pastime being contrary to our forward-looking, progressive society. The decades-long marginalization of American history in the nation's public schools was a reflection of that, Hitchens concluded; this was perhaps the most telling evidence that we as a people (or *peoples*) were not truly invested in our past despite all the TV shows, movies, and monuments suggesting otherwise.[48]

David McCullough, the author of a number of best sellers and the most popular American historian of the day, ironically agreed that people in this country were much more interested in the future than the past. For McCullough, however, history was the most exciting of subjects because it was ultimately about people, and there was nothing more fascinating than people, whether they lived in the present or the past. McCullough even challenged the notion of there being a "past" in that people always lived in their own present. History was the study of different "presents," he explained in a 1999 television interview, an interesting way to think about the subject that could perhaps help Americans—especially young people—appreciate it more. The key to writing or teaching history, according to McCullough, was avoiding the tendency to describe it as preordained—that is, that things did not have to turn out the way they did. Maintaining a sense that anything could have happened, which was true, was the best way to keep readers and students invested in a story, he revealed, recommending an almost "whodunit" approach to history.[49]

Getting the last word in on American history in the twentieth century were perhaps Roy Rosenzweig and David Thelen in their 1998 book *The Presence of the Past*, in which they took issue with those suggesting we were predominantly a present- and future-focused people and challenged conservatives' claims that our national identity was getting lost in a sea of multiculturalism. Americans were very connected to the past, they reported, and just not in the way we think they were or should be. The authors' findings were based on a research poll in which a national sample of Americans was asked about the role the past (rather than history) played in their everyday lives. Most Americans were heavily invested in the past in all kinds of ways, the study showed, doing everything from preserving photographs and videos, holding family reunions, collecting antiques, and working on family genealogies. Americans were also avid consumers of the past, using television, movies, books, and museums to find compelling stories from yesterday. American history in the traditional sense was largely off their radar, with little knowledge of or interest in the things to be found in the subject's textbooks. American history was boring and irrelevant, it could be said, while the American past, especially that related to their personal lives, was positively fascinating.[50]

Given these findings, were we thinking about American history in the wrong way? Was the nation's history—that is, the "American narrative"— more important than individuals' own history and stories from the past that they found meaningful in some way? In their respective afterwords, Rosenzweig and Thelen each proposed building a bridge between peoples' personal pasts and American history, this perhaps being the only way to rescue the field from both its political battles and low status within the education arena. Such an approach could perhaps even lead to the "usable past" historians viewed as the holy grail of the field, a best-case scenario with which all parties would be pleased. As we turned the corner into a new century, however, American history remained a contentious site, with no holy grail to be discovered in the foreseeable future.[51]

# 6 The Fray of History

2000–

> Whatever the cause, we may be witnessing an epidemic of amnesia,
> global in scale, with potentially profound social and political conse-
> quences. In losing our history, we may be simultaneously losing our
> future, not only as a nation, but as a race.
> Stephen Bertman, "America Is Suffering from Cultural Amnesia"

In 2001, just a couple of months after 9/11, in fact, the findings of a recent
Gallup poll of American college seniors were reported in the media. Just
as in 1943, when the *New York Times* found in its own survey that college
freshmen were deficient in American history, this poll revealed that higher
education students of the early twenty-first century were not very well
acquainted with their country's past. Forty-two percent could not place
the Civil War within the half century in which it took place, for example;
this particular finding sadly contradicted President Abraham Lincoln's
remark in his 1863 Gettysburg Address, "The world . . . can never forget
what [occurred] here." Unfortunately, as yet another recent survey has
shown, that statistic was not a random glitch in students' historical memory. Almost a quarter of twelve- to seventeen-year-olds surveyed by the
Colonial Williamsburg Foundation in 2001 were not aware that the Civil
War was fought between the North and South; 13 percent believed it was
a war between the United States and England, while 5 percent thought
it was a struggle between the U.S. East and West. The teens were more
knowledgeable about which parties were involved in the Revolutionary
War but, even so, almost a fifth of them got it wrong: 14 percent were of

the mind that we had declared independence from France, 3 percent from Native Americans, and 1 percent from Canada.[1]

Much had changed in the United States in the years between the *New York Times* survey and the ones conducted in 2001, but apparently not so when it came to the subject of American history. Both high school and college students—our best and brightest hope for the future—were historically challenged, if not historically illiterate, and this was cause for considerable alarm among those who believed that a firm grasp of American history was a fundamental part of citizenship and national identity. As it had for much of the twentieth century, this concern would continue to haunt American education in the early twenty-first as a frightening presence that refused to go away. Like the world wars, however, a cataclysmic event would soon thrust history into the national consciousness, the need to look back always magnified in times of emergency. For the first time, in fact, a concerted effort was launched to try to fix America's history problem, an initiative that can now be seen as having mixed results. History remains a problem in American education, but there are signs of hope on the horizon, good news for a field that has served as a lightning rod for controversy for almost the past century.

## The Social Equivalent of Alzheimer's Disease

As might be expected, critics found the results of the recent history quizzes both depressing and distressing. Yet another one, fielded by the American Council of Trustees and Alumni in 2000, revealed that 81 percent of graduating seniors at the country's best colleges could not pass a basic test of American historical knowledge. The report so infuriated Senator Robert C. Byrd of West Virginia that he convinced his colleagues to add $50 million to the U.S. Department of Education's fiscal year 2001 appropriations bill for "programs to teach American history," with another $100 million to come in 2002.[2] Byrd's passion and political clout would over the next decade transform the field through sponsored programs designed to support professional development seminars for precollegiate teachers of history, a good example of how a single individual can trigger a true social movement.

Meanwhile, however, educators made their worries known upon hearing the results of the latest surveys. Even some living outside the United States were upset by the news. For example, Stephen Bertman, a professor at the University of Windsor in Ontario, Canada, was deeply disturbed by the findings of the recent polls, arguing that Americans' lack of knowledge of the nation's past was nothing less than a form of "cultural amnesia." Writing in USA Today magazine in 2001, Bertman went as far as to say that our historical forgetfulness was "the social equivalent of Alzheimer's disease," which was quite a statement. "Debilitating and progressive," he wrote, "the malady is eating away at America's soul, for just as an individual needs memories to maintain a sense of personal identity, so does a nation need them in order to survive."[3]

For Bertman it was the loss of continuity that was so troubling about Americans' skimpy knowledge of their own history. The awareness that America's story was a continuing one, rooted in the past but pointing to the future, was essential if the nation was to realize its full potential. It could be understood if Americans forgot or never knew important names and dates in history, but an unfamiliarity with the fundamental themes of the nation's story was inexcusable. The accelerated pace of society had something to do with the loss of interest in what had happened some time ago, Bertman proposed, as did the explosion of information via digital technology. Simply put, "now" had eclipsed "then," a process carrying serious consequences. Besides better teaching of the subject, there were some things Americans could do to restore the memory of their past, Bertman believed. Reading historical literature, visiting art museums, listening to classical music, and even watching old films would make people more history-conscious, he suggested—a step in the right direction. Simply displaying photographs of older relatives, telling family stories to children, and keeping ethnic and religious traditions alive would serve the same purpose, with all of this designed to bring more of yesterday into today.[4]

Bruce Cole, chairman of the National Endowment for the Humanities, agreed that Americans were facing a serious threat of "amnesia." In a talk at New York University titled "The Urgency of Memory," Cole pointed out that a common thread of any great civilization was an awareness of its past, something clearly lacking in contemporary society. It was not enough to justify our loss of memory by reiterating that we were a forward-looking people more concerned with what happens tomorrow than what happened yesterday. A keen vision of the future relied on a thorough view of the past, Cole explained, with this perhaps being the most important role of history. "We cannot see clearly ahead if we are blind to history," he said, citing some of the disheartening results of the recent tests given to students. (The National Assessment of Education Progress had just found that over half of high school seniors could not identify our enemies in World War II.) "Such collective amnesia is dangerous," Cole told the audience, thinking that an ignorance of one's heritage was not just poor preparation for the future but led to an inability to understand and appreciate other cultures.[5]

Cole's words certainly made sense, but the truth was that only world-shattering occurrences typically had a direct, immediate impact on stirring up Americans' historical consciousness. Like Pearl Harbor, the attacks of September 11, 2001, did just that, raising all kinds of questions about the links between the country's past and present. One such question—asked by Joshua Zeitz in *American Heritage* a few months after the attacks—was, "Are our liberties in peril?" Zeitz placed the horrific event and its aftermath in historical perspective, addressing concerns about the new kinds of governmental scrutiny being put into place. Personal liberties and collective security were indeed a tricky balancing act, he explained, especially during wartime. There was no doubt that war emergencies of the past resulted in a curtailing of America's freedoms. As President George W. Bush did in some cases, President Lincoln suspended habeas corpus (the right of a person under arrest to be brought before a court or judge) during the Civil War, for example, an act ruled to be unconstitutional by a Supreme Court chief justice. (Lincoln ignored the ruling.) President Woodrow Wilson, meanwhile, exhibited little tolerance for socialists and even labor unions during World War I—or, in fact, anyone who did not subscribe to the idea of "100 percent Americanism," a clear violation of freedom of speech. It was, however, the detainment of Japanese Americans during World War II that represented the most egregious example of an officially endorsed taking away of liberties. Although none of this was good news, Zeitz was happy to report that the nation's commitment to freedoms was not only restored after each war but strengthened—words of comfort as talk of wiretapping and other forms of domestic surveillance made headlines in late 2001.[6]

Roger Rosenblatt of *Time* agreed that 9/11 had thrust America back into what he termed "the fray of history." Writing two months after the attacks, Rosenblatt made the intriguing argument that for the previous dozen years (since the end of the Cold War), the United States had been "living outside history," meaning there had been little need for Americans to be concerned with the larger sweep of time. But now history was back with a vengeance, demanding a look back in order to make some sense of the tragic events of the day. September 11 was a reminder that no nation, regardless of its power or wealth, should forget its past lest it experience a false sense of security. The world could be a very dangerous place, we were reminded, and it was a lesson we hopefully would not soon forget.[7]

While Pearl Harbor was most often cited, other "terrorist" events of the past were recalled to historicize 9/11. Almost a century earlier, for example, there was a bombing in New York's financial district (the result ing damage to what had been the J. P. Morgan building at Wall and Broad Streets can still be seen), a terrorist attack committed by unnamed radicals that was the most deadly in American history until the Oklahoma City blast in 1995. On September 16, 1920, a horse cart filled with dynamite and weights exploded, killing thirty and injuring three hundred. (Forty people would ultimately die from the bombing.) With a violent explosion, a black column of smoke, and people on fire in downtown Manhattan, "9/16" was similar to 9/11, although of course on a much smaller scale. If there were any positives to be gained by being reminded of the event, it was that Wall Street opened the very next day in 1920, an intentional act to demonstrate that terrorism could win a battle but never the war.[8]

The events of 9/11 had an immediate and direct impact on the already much maligned subject of American history. As during and after the two world wars, academics, particularly more conservative ones, called for more and better teaching of American history, thinking that this would somehow help buttress us against future attacks (or even prevent them). Teaching and learning the subject would necessarily involve an examination of the concepts of freedom and religious tolerance, it was felt, with such instruction instilling among students a greater pride in our nation and its core principles. Historians such as Eric Foner of Columbia University pondered how the upsurge of patriotism following 9/11 would shape the subject over the long term, again using the past to help predict the future. Previous wars, such as the one in Vietnam, prompted historians to reevaluate the symbols that represented the country and its values, something that was already happening a year after the 9/11 attacks. As well, a closer study of the nation's relationship with the international community was a natural by-product of a foreign war, and this was an area in which historians were spending considerable time. If there was one danger to postwar histories, particularly among conservatives, it was the tendency to put self-celebration ahead of critical analysis, causing Foner to caution his colleagues against taking a self-absorbed approach.[9]

## Democracy in America

The nation's reentering the fray of history after 9/11 had many angles, of course, but proved to resurrect the work of one man in particular: Alexis de Tocqueville. As if a switch had been pulled, a flurry of attention was given to Tocqueville's classic *Democracy in America*, a response also perhaps to the unknowns of a new century and new millennium. A new translation of the work (originally published in two volumes in 1835 and 1840) had just been published, and this certainly contributed to the Tocqueville fever of the early years of the twenty-first century. The book was even relevant to the 2000 presidential race between Al Gore and George W. Bush, Robert J. Samuelson of *Newsweek* thought, suggesting that the Frenchman would not have been surprised at all by the bitterness of the campaign. (Early nineteenth-century politics were hardly congenial.) Tocqueville's ghost tended to reappear at any major juncture in the country's history, in fact, his words viewed as both a soothing reminder of our indestructible national character and insightful critique of our fundamental flaws.[10]

As the new century rolled on, Tocqueville continued to garner attention as others realized how remarkable and visionary *Democracy in America* truly was. Some considered it to be the greatest book about the United States, even though it was written just a half century after the nation's founding. The book's central theme—that America was the most unique country in the world—continued to reverberate in the twenty-first century, a reaction one might say to the nation's less certain role on the global stage. The American middle class was stalled, but the middle classes of Brazil, China, India, and Russia were beginning to boom, raising serious questions about the nation's future in a new world order. Likewise, the American Dream appeared to be more difficult to achieve than ever, but many foreigners were enjoying the fruits of upward mobility. Tocqueville's book thus also served as an ideal benchmark to test the America of then versus now and measure whether our original greatness and uniqueness still existed.[11]

Tocqueville was not the only figure of American history to make a major comeback in the early twenty-first century. John Adams had also become quite the sensation, a result of David McCullough's 751-page biography of him in 2001. One would not think that the second president of the United States would make good beach reading, but the book was a best seller during the summer of that year, the man's surly demeanor and romantic relationship with his wife Abigail a popular topic at swanky soirees. How to explain the Adams phenomenon beyond McCullough's excellent writing skills and Simon and Schuster's first-rate marketing campaign for the book? Wilfred M. McClay, a professor at the University of Tennessee, had some theories, challenging the accepted notion that Americans were not a history-minded people. Contrary to popular belief, Americans had a deep affinity for history, he argued, rejecting the standard trope that our progressive, practical view of the world negated a need or desire to know much about the past. "A considerable part of the American public actually has a broad and sustained hunger for history and has repeatedly shown that it will respond generously to an accessible, graceful work about an important subject by a trusted and admired author," McClay wrote in *Wilson's Quarterly* in 2001, adding that we "yearn for solid knowledge of [our] nation's origins, which in a real sense are [our] own origins too." For most Americans, history was not "more or less bunk," as Henry Ford famously said, positing instead that a meaningful connection to the past was an essential part of our national character.[12]

To support his claim McClay pointed to the abundance of ways Americans celebrated or "consumed" history, both past and present. The U.S. bicentennial was perhaps the perfect example—particularly the procession of tall ships through New York harbor. Ken Burns's 1990 documentary *The Civil War* was another blast of American history into the public's consciousness, achieving a level of popularity that McClay believed exceeded that of any "professional" (i.e., scholarly) historian. The attention recently given to "the greatest generation" was also history at its best, he felt, with Tom Brokaw's 1998 titular best seller, the film *Saving Private Ryan* that same year, the 2000 founding of the D-Day Museum (now the National WWII Museum) in New Orleans, the 2001 television miniseries *Band of Brothers*, and planning for the World War II Memorial in Washington DC all part of the phenomenon. (Clint Eastwood's 2006 *Flags of Our Fathers* also kept interest in World War II and "the greatest generation" very much alive later in the decade.) Hitting the nail on the head, McClay insisted that Americans had no interest in historical "factoids and tales" but were enchanted by stories from the past "from which they can draw meaning and sustenance, and in which their own identity is deeply embedded."[13]

Indeed, although the academic arena of American history remained politicized and problematic, the field as a whole remained healthy as we crossed over into the twenty-first century. Rather than just argue how the subject should be taught, American historians and those outside the field focused on how it could be used. In his 2000 best seller *The Tipping Point*, for example, Malcolm Gladwell discussed "why Paul Revere's message stuck," finding useful applications for this particular site of American history. The subject was also increasingly seen as a valuable resource by businesspeople, who added American history to their tool kits as a predictive device when making decisions about the future. Interest in genealogy also exploded in the early years of the new century, making American history suddenly rather fashionable. Two trends—the graying of baby boomers and the making available of immigration and census records online—were largely responsible for an ongoing boom in genealogy. Families tracing their ancestral roots could not help but bump into historical events, after all, and this became a great example of how to construct a "usable past" on an individual level. Through two PBS series produced later in the decade featuring celebrities, *Faces of America* and *Finding Your Roots*, Henry Louis Gates Jr. championed the idea of Americans learning more about who they were by constructing a family tree as far back as was possible. Another show on NBC, *Who Do You Think You Are?*, did much the same, also illustrating that American history is, at its best, personal.

## No Child Left Behind

While American history enjoyed good times in popular culture, the field continued to struggle in the nation's schools. Educators who had taught U.S. history at the high school or university level for decades were perhaps most qualified to determine how the field had changed over time, almost always not for the better. The consensus was that the teaching of American history had steadily declined since the 1960s if students' preparation in and aptitude for the subject was the primary measure. This was certainly the view of one such educator, Theodore K. Rabb of Princeton University, who had more than forty years of teaching college students under his belt. The encroachment of contemporary issues, particularly foreign affairs, had gradually chipped away at the foundation of American history, he felt, leaving students without a solid understanding of the nation's rich past. Nonacademic pursuits—notably, sports and community service— had also infringed on students' time, with less "practical" subjects like history becoming the biggest victims. Test after test confirmed all this, becoming the impetus for concerned parties—notably, Senator Byrd—to try to rectify the situation.[14]

Countering such noble efforts, however, was the No Child Left Behind Act signed by President Bush in 2002. The act mandated states to set standards for teachers' qualifications and for students' aptitude in reading and mathematics, to determine progress in those areas, and to allocate funds accordingly. With money at stake based on performance in reading and math, school districts almost by default made other subjects, such as history, less of a priority. More broadly, No Child Left Behind had the effect of turning the classroom experience into a pursuit for good test scores, with the financial incentive for such being difficult to resist. Good test scores, if they were achieved, however, were something quite different from academic substance and critical thinking. "Increasingly, Americans are being taught skills, not content," Rabb remarked, his experience suggesting that students were "being trained, not educated."[15] American history, already weakened from decades of dilution, was further enervated by No Child Left Behind, leaving it all but a shell of what it had once been. Even social studies was taking a backseat to math, reading, and often science, and sometimes it was taught only when time permitted.[16] Including history as a test subject (as some countries, including the Netherlands, did) would go a long way toward rescuing the subject, but that possibility was not even being discussed by anyone with the power to make it happen.

Nothing, arguably, pointed to the trouble in teaching and learning American history more than Jon Stewart's mock textbook, *America (the Book): A Citizen's Guide to Democracy Inaction*. A send-up of the books used in social studies classes that had no apparent motive to get students to think critically (it was presented as a "Teacher's Edition"), *America (the Book)* was either loved or hated by those taking the time to read it. Written in the same wink-wink style as Stewart's *The Daily Show*, the book ridiculed the overt identity politics of the times, making the quite serious point that actual learning was being left out in the process. Some, however, were not amused at all by Stewart's book. R. Emmett Tyrell Jr., editor of the conservative *American Spectator*, thought the fake textbook was in very bad taste, so bad in fact that it earned his dubious J. Gordon Coogler Award for the Worst Book of the Year. Tyrell found the author's satiric interpretation of American history decidedly unfunny. "Though Ronald Reagan (1980–1989) was not Kennedyesque, many historians believe he was among our most Reaganesque commanders-in-chief," went one quip that Tyrell found more infantile than droll.[17]

For those who did not appreciate Stewart's sense of humor, there was Thomas Woods's *The Politically Incorrect Guide to American History*.

Also a best seller, the book was an alternative, decidedly conservative reading of the nation's past, it too a response of sorts to the don't-offend-anyone approach of contemporary social studies textbooks. Unlike Stewart, however, Woods was being perfectly serious, maintaining that the books were not just inclusive to a fault but politically leftist. The Puritans were not racists, the Founding Fathers were not revolutionaries, the Civil War was not about slavery, and Franklin Delano Roosevelt did not get the country out of the Depression, Woods asserted, adding that these were the usual accepted beliefs grounded in the liberal revisionism that had run amuck over the course of the last generation.[18] Textbooks used to teach American history to high school students were being attacked from both left and right, an indication that nobody except the profit-making publishers were happy with what was in them.

## Teaching American History

While politically charged critiques of American history helped elevate the travails of the field in the public's mind, a check for hundreds of millions of dollars promised to create real change. Although obviously justified to be in the nation's best interests, the Teaching American History (TAH) program could be said to have been a pet project of Byrd. As he told his colleagues from the Senate floor in May 2001, Byrd's study of American heroes (particularly Nathan Hale) had a deep impact on him while growing up in the West Virginia coalfields. Byrd could see a bigger world through the lens of the heroes' lives from which he gained a lifelong love for the history of the country, he explained in an emotional appeal that was difficult to dismiss. Senators on both sides of the aisle were no doubt moved by Byrd's story, one to which those elected to public office could likely relate.[19]

The TAH program formally began that year with the mission of providing teachers of U.S. history with content that they could subsequently pass on to their students. Partnering with people and institutions having expertise in the subject (colleges, universities, historical societies, archives, and museums) was an essential piece of the program, which offered three-year federal education grants up to $1 million to school districts lucky enough to land one. (The grants were awarded after a national competition, with sixty school districts in forty-five states and the District of

Columbia recipients in 2001, and 114 grants in thirty-nine states and the District of Columbia in 2002.) Ironically, the TAH program became part of the No Child Left Behind Act, which had arguably done much to marginalize American history in the nation's schools. Wisely, however, social studies curricula (often intended to be "content-free") were not included in the program, offering American history teachers the all too rare opportunity to focus on their subject of choice. With American history undervalued in most elementary and secondary schools, teachers often lacking adequate knowledge in the subject (55 percent of those who taught history neither majored or minored in the subject while in college, Diane Ravitch found[20]), and students performing poorly on standardized tests, the TAH program was nothing less than a godsend for the field. "The program is alive and well and off to a good start," reported Alex Stein in *The History Teacher* in February 2003, happy to see this "bold new idea" gain traction.[21]

Experiences with the TAH grant project flooded history education journals through the decade, with each author, often a high school or college teacher, telling his or her own personal story. For example, Stan Pesick and Shelley Weintraub of the Oakland, California, Unified School District used their TAH grant to explore what they called "DeTocqueville's [*sic*] ghost"—that is, how democracy in America had evolved since the Frenchman wrote his book. Examining that seminal issue would help teachers and ultimately students develop a greater historical understanding, believed Pesick, Weintraub, and a group of historians from the University of California–Berkeley, and that was deemed important for their school district. Students there did not generally perform well on assessments in American history (and other subjects), and recruiting and keeping credentialed teachers was not easy. Teachers worked with the historians to gain content that was subsequently translated into "lesson studies," a two-phased process that achieved the team's objective. Teachers found they shared the same, fundamental goal of university professors—passing on knowledge of history to young people—and it was a realization that helped make the subject more exciting for both them and their students.[22]

The Oakland case study was a prime example of how American history could be reinvigorated even in challenging academic environments. Sema Brainin, a professor at Hunter College in New York, applied a federally funded TAH grant to change the culture of American history in East Harlem middle schools, an equally daunting mission. Partnering with the New York City Department of Education, the local community school district, and the Museum of the City of New York (MCNY), Brainin focused less on curricula than on how to attract, train, and retain good teachers at the seventh and eighth grade levels. History teachers typically did not last long in the district, and those who did had to deal with the mandate of raising test scores in reading and math and the concomitant neglect of social studies. For its three-year TAH project, the team wisely tapped into the plethora of history content available in public venues in the city, something that had surprisingly not been done by that district's teachers. Ten teachers attended lectures given by notable historians at the New York Public Library's Gilder Lehrman Institute and at MCNY, an opportunity to engage in world-class scholarship. Seminars followed the lectures, during which the teachers had the chance to share ideas with each other and, more generally, "talk history." Through their grant, the East Harlem teachers felt like "real," professional historians, deepening their commitment to remain in the district.[23]

While improving the teaching of American history was the primary goal of TAH, students also benefited from direct exposure to "professional" historians. For the Waukegan, Illinois, school district, Rachel G. Ragland of Lake Forest College partnered with the Chicago Historical Society, a collaboration that helped both students and teachers take a different attitude toward and view of the subject. Their three-year program led to a new way to teach the traditional American history survey course, specifically by having practicing historians present "content knowledge" to high school students. Students were thus first shown how to "do history" and "think historically" before teachers translated that content into pedagogical terms, a two-phased approach that was very effective. Lectures and textbook readings were de-emphasized, replaced by the use of primary documents and Internet research, small group activities, and a focus on interpretation versus the memorization of facts. Not only did students find history to be more "alive" and personally relevant, but teachers felt more confident about their own mastery of the subject.[24]

Ragland, along with Kelly A. Woestman, ended up editing a book about the TAH project that served as a history of Senator Byrd's "bold new idea." Published in 2009 (two years before the TAH program ended), *The Teaching American History Project: Lessons for Educators and Historians* was an assessment of what turned out to be the biggest infusion of federal dollars into K–12 history education in this country. More than $1 billion had already been distributed via more than a thousand grants of about $1 million each. Was the $1 billion well spent? Contributors to the book (all participants in TAH grants) certainly thought so, believing that the funding was instrumental in bridging the gap between teachers and professional historians. Museum educators also benefited by learning ways to get middle school students excited about their exhibits, and university professors had a new understanding of how remaining in their ivory tower was not good for the field in the larger scheme of things. TAH programs made teachers' jobs much more fun, the (clearly partial) audit showed, the opportunity to get out of their classrooms making them more committed when they were in them.[25]

### An Ongoing Conversation about the Past

Even with the TAH grant, however, changing the conventional ways in which American history was taught to children was not easy, as Wilson J. Warren of Western Michigan University in Kalamazoo found. Textbooks and ancillary materials—worksheets, maps, study guides, and the like—were firmly entrenched in elementary and secondary schools, making the pursuit of having students "do history" or "think historically" a more ambitious undertaking. Many teachers at that level believed that using historical documents in the classroom and adopting an interpretative approach to subject matter were wonderful ideas, but they were reluctant to actually put them into practice. Because of the looming state-directed social studies assessment or merit exam, teachers often had to cover the entire history of the United States in their courses, a task that made it impossible to dig deep into any particular topic or use innovative methods.[26]

At the college level, however, more professors were eagerly abandoning the "coverage" approach wherever possible for alternative pedagogical strategies that paid bigger dividends in terms of student learning. David J. Voelker of the University of Wisconsin–Green Bay was one historian not interested in what he called "coverage for coverage's sake," finding a different and more effective way to teach his introductory U.S. history course. Memorization of "what happened" was the wrong way to study history, Voelker felt, with the two basic conduits of information—lectures and textbooks—only reinforcing the bad technique. Using more primary and secondary sources was useful toward developing an interpretive versus factual model, he found, as was a deep dive into controversial topics (e.g., church versus state and freedom of speech). Understanding history rested primarily on the realization that historians are engaged in "an ongoing conversation about the past," Voelker wrote in *The History Teacher*, the construction of narratives a better way of learning than the standard get-from-point-A-to-point-B-as-fast-as-possible method of teaching introductory or survey courses.[27]

Innovation in teaching American history to college students was also born out of necessity, other professors found. Learning on the very first day of class that his students "hated" U.S. history, Schaun Wheeler of the University of Connecticut realized he had to revise his syllabus very quickly. That he did, throwing out two staples of the field—a chronological approach and the focus on particular groups and people. Instead, Wheeler took a three-pronged approach that took a roundabout but much more likable way for students to take the time and effort to learn the subject. The first step was to point out what Wheeler described as "patterns" in society—in this case, Black English Vernacular (BEV). The second step was to connect those patterns to social institutions (the ban on BEV in Oakland schools), and the third to connect those institutions to history (the link between anti-BEV sentiment and slavery). "They could see the origins of aspects of the world that they could actually observe today," Wheeler happily reported, the connection between present individuals and society and those of the past being the vital piece of the equation that was missing from typical history classes. Class participation rose, students more critically evaluated assigned readings, and learning outside of class increased, all things any teacher wishes for. Best of all, perhaps, students were less sure of what to believe about American history, adopting a healthy skepticism of what was accepted as "truth."[28]

Despite all the recent success stories in the teaching of American history, often framed within the larger field of social studies, the dynamics of the field have remained one of the biggest and emotionally charged issues within the nation's education system. Kevin St. Jarre, a social studies teacher at Fort Kent Community High School in Maine, created somewhat of a row with his 2008 essay in *Phi Delta Kappan*, illustrating how passionate some K–12 educators felt about the messy situation. St. Jarre made what appeared to be a reasonable argument: more discussion, reading, writing, and analysis were needed in social studies classrooms, as facts, figures, and dates did not do justice to American history. Depth, not breadth, was the key to good history, he suggested, meaning that other social sciences—international studies, sociology, economics, civics, philosophy, ethics, psychology, and more—necessarily had to be woven into the process. "Any historian who chooses to do truly thorough analysis must leave history behind and march unswervingly into one of the other social sciences," he wrote, the subject by nature being an interdisciplinary one. St. Jarre was a firm believer in the social studies curriculum, and only this approach was able to inform American history with the proper context and perspective it required and deserved.[29]

Judging by the response to the high school teacher's essay, however, one might think that St. Jarre had proposed eliminating American history from higher education altogether. Robert B. Bain, a professor at the University of Michigan who had taught high school social studies in the Cleveland area for a quarter century, felt that St. Jarre had made "a bad argument for a reasonable position." When taught properly, history was not chronology and the subject was not presented in a vacuum, Bain made clear, citing evidence to the contrary. Eleventh grade American history teachers routinely structured the subject within a political, economic, or social framework by linking current issues to the past. As well, historical inquiry was a common device, the use of questions often employed to open up discussions about key events and movements of yesterday. Eighth grade teachers also went far beyond an encyclopedic recitation of history in their classrooms, Bain insisted, frequently employing the Socratic method to stimulate critical thinking and illuminate ideas. Far from being a narrow and shallow subject when left to itself without its social studies cousins, he insisted, American history was a robust one that took students down some interesting paths and expanded their vision of the world.[30]

## The Joy of History

Nobody had to tell that to the most popular historian in this country, David McCullough. In recent years, in fact, no one more than McCullough has served as a better spokesman for American history, the man acting as the unofficial ambassador for the field. Along with documentarian (and frequent collaborator) Ken Burns, McCullough has made the most compelling arguments for why Americans should know their country's history. For the author (a two-time winner of both the Pulitzer Prize and the National Book Award), history served a vital purpose for both the individual and larger society. "Learning about history is an antidote to the hubris of the present, the idea that everything in our lives is the ultimate," he wrote in *American Heritage* in 2008, indicating that no subject was better equipped to provide us with a sense of perspective—that is, the ability to know what is important and what is not.[31]

After writing a number of best sellers—notably, *John Adams, 1776,* and *Truman*—McCullough was on a mission to rectify what he saw as the historical illiteracy of young Americans. A regular on the college lecture circuit, McCullough was taken aback by some university students' glaring ignorance of American history. When following one of his talks one student remarked that she had not known that all thirteen colonies were on the East Coast, McCullough had had enough. Educators, parents, and writers had to do a better job of communicating to the younger generation the idea that one could not know where one was going if one did not know where one has been. The same held true for a nation, he was convinced, meaning the destiny of the United States rested heavily on a thorough familiarity with the past. Although there were some very good reasons to receive a solid education in American history—most notably the likelihood of creating better citizens and more understanding human beings—McCullough believed the subject should be taught and learned simply because it was pleasurable. "The joy of history, like art or music or literature, consists of an expansion of the experience of being alive," he concluded, and a more convincing rationale is difficult to conceive.[32]

James W. Loewen, author of *Lies My Teacher Told Me*, was fine with history being joyous as long as it was truthful. Textbooks failed to do that, he believed, and this was a disservice to students who deserved better. Loewen, a sociologist, had certainly done his homework, spending two years at the Smithsonian Institution to survey the dozen top-selling American history textbooks. The books had no shortage of nationalism, optimism, and, less fortunately, misinformation, the books themselves receiving a failing grade. "Textbooks suggest that we've always tried to do the right thing," he told an interviewer for *Phi Delta Kappan* in 2010, and this was a lie that was not just bad history but worsened relationships both here and abroad. Race relations and foreign policy each suffered because of this untruth, Loewen argued, and were a good example of how history was directly relevant to the present. Publishers deliberately sanitized textbooks in order not to lose sales, he felt, with the truth about certain figures or events still hard to take by some where regional sentiment ran strong. (Which side won the Civil War was a contended issue in some circles, rather amazingly, with some sympathetic to the Southern cause certain that the Confederacy was the victor.)[33]

Covering up the truth to avoid offending textbook buyers necessarily resulted in blandness, and this ultimately turned young people off to the field. A not-so-well-kept secret was that the authors of American history textbooks were often not the actual writers; the arduous task of putting words to paper was frequently farmed out to anonymous academics in order to save time and money. (Some authors had not even read the books on which their names appeared.) Abandon the textbook, Loewen urged teachers of the subject, thinking most educators would be better off creating their own curriculum from scratch.[34] In a follow-up of sorts to *Lies My Teacher Told Me*, Loewen wrote *Teaching What Really Happened*, a how-to for teachers to get students excited about "doing" history. Loewen recommended a project-oriented, self-learning form of historiography focusing on the American Indian experience, slavery, and race relations, an alternative approach to what he called the "tyranny" of textbooks.[35]

Conservatives in Texas, ironically, also believed that most American history textbooks were filled with lies. Forty years after Norma and Mel Gabler pressured publishers to avoid a liberal bias lest school districts drop their books like hot potatoes, Texas remained the home of pro-evolution, pro-Christian, and pro-Reagan educational activism. Now, in 2010, it was Don McLeroy who was leading the crusade, using his seat on the Texas State Board of Education to infuse ultraconservative values into the textbook selection process. For McLeroy and his allies, Senator Joseph McCarthy had not been that bad, global-warming was a bunch of hooey, and the civil rights movement was not that big of a deal—these being just some of the ideas he believed American history textbooks should incorporate. Because of its size, Texas still influenced what school districts across the country decided, making the ultra-right-wing faction there especially powerful.[36]

The McLeroy contingent in Texas had a truly remarkable interpretation of the nation's past: slavery was a remnant of British colonialism rather than an active cog in America's economic machine; Muslims were a naturally aggressive people; and our political system was more accurately described as "republican" versus "democratic." As coiner of the phrase "separation between church and state," Thomas Jefferson was a dangerous person, he and his radical ideas better left out of textbooks.[37] U.S. Supreme Court Justice Thurgood Marshall and labor leader Cesar Chavez were also persona non grata, and this was clearly an attempt to de-emphasize the contributions of people of color. America was not only a Christian nation but a white nation, McLeroy and his colleagues believed; this despite the fact that pluralism was an integral element of the very motto of the country. Not just nationalism but arrogance streamed through the group's agenda, with a view of history that bordered on fascism. The United States was "not only unique but superior," McLeroy proudly stated, its people "divinely ordained to lead the world to betterment."[38] Thankfully, a backlash against McLeroyism is growing, as even run-of-the-mill Republicans view its hate-filled politics as more of a liability than an asset for the party.[39]

## The Future of History

The power of ultraconservatives to dictate textbook content was an indication that, despite the recent progress made in the field, all was not well in American history. While many teachers had a greater mastery of the subject—the result of the TAH grant and innovative pedagogy—students overall did not appear to have made equivalent gains. History repeated itself, one could say, when yet another study showed that America's youth were less than fluent in the nation's past. The 2011 test given to students of various grade levels across the country produced findings as alarming as any of the other history quizzes administered over the decades. Less than half of fourth graders were not aware of the significance of Abraham Lincoln's presidency, and just 2 percent of high school seniors could identify the central issue of the *Brown v. Board of Education* case addressed by the Supreme Court in 1954. While the old standby—poor teaching—was commonly pointed to as the source of the problem, others continued to argue that the math-and-science-heavy No Child Left Behind curriculum was mainly to blame. Some, however, were not at all surprised by the results of the test, knowing that this was hardly a new story. Americans never knew that much about their history, it was safe to say, and our interest in what was before us or coming around the corner was far greater than what had already come and gone.[40]

As always, however, our apathy if not antipathy toward American history as an academic subject was in stark contrast to our relationship with it when encountered in popular culture. The popularity of history-based television channels, documentary films, and local historical societies were all good examples of how history was thriving from an entertainment or leisure sensibility, as John Lukacs pointed out in *The Future of History*, and it was a curious thing given how unpopular the subject appeared to be in school. Historical nonfiction sold better than novels, additional evidence that Americans really liked history when it was presented a certain way. One had to wonder whether young people were simply averse to learning history; was the subject appreciated only by those of a certain age? Or was it a pedagogical issue, meaning the methods of teaching the subject were still largely flawed? Either way, American history remained somewhat of a conundrum, with few answers forthcoming regarding how to bridge the gap between the subject's favorable status in "applied" settings and its unfavorable one within higher education.[41]

After some fifteen years of trying to solve the American history riddle, one professor believed he had figured out why the subject was the runt of the litter in academia yet a big moneymaker in the world of commerce. The most important part of history—the story—was glaringly absent in the country's education system, Lendol Calder of Augustana College in Illinois proposed, and this was the root cause of the problem. Every year Calder asked his students to write a brief, impromptu history of the United States to determine what they used as a guiding framework for the nation's past. Consistently, most students used no framework whatsoever, thinking our history was essentially just one event followed by another. Without some kind of grand narrative, students had no real conception of story when it came to history, and this accounted for the lack of interest and low test scores in the subject. Given the enjoyment of the subject in popular culture, Calder's theory made a lot of sense; story was paramount in the entertainment universe, something educators apparently should literally go to school on.[42]

Niall Ferguson, the popular Harvard University historian and author, was similarly motivated to crack the code of American history in order to get young people interested in their country's amazing past. Ferguson was a devout member of the "history matters" school, not happy that 38 percent of a representative sample of Americans recently failed the test given to immigrants for citizenship. A firm believer that the past informed the present, in 2011 he asked how one could fully appreciate our unique set of freedoms if one had little idea of how, when, and why they developed. All states required high school students to have some kind of instruction in American history, begging the question of how our education system produced so many adults who were functionally illiterate in the subject.[43]

Ferguson, best known for his unusually engaging historical books, put the blame not on teachers but squarely on textbooks. The leading high school textbook in the subject was Pearson Education's *United*

*States History*, which ran over twelve hundred pages, weighed over six pounds, and cost over $100. "How much would you love history if you had to carry one of those to school every day?" he asked, noting that the book's boringness exceeded its heft. Publishers' two main objectives—comprehensiveness and political correctness—were simply antithetical to a good narrative, Ferguson maintained; the fact that the books were team written and committee approved made them more like nonalphabetized encyclopedias than descriptive histories. Academics' specialization was another big problem; authors of the books were typically unable to identify and express the larger, more important themes of historical events and their long-term consequences. Ferguson had a couple of suggestions for making American history a subject more high school students would like to learn about. First, replace those massive tomes with interactive web-based content, mimicking one of teens' favorite activities—online games. Second, ask more "what if" questions to get students thinking, trading upon a recent trend in fiction. What if FDR had not been president during World War II? Philip Roth had asked in his 2004 *The Plot against America*, just the kind of query that could encourage young people to accept the notion that nothing in history was preordained.[44]

Over the last few years, even more innovative pedagogical strategies have been employed to get students interested in American history. For example, Katherine G. Aiken, professor of history at the University of Idaho, has used comic books as a way to teach the subject, finding them to be an effective device for illustrating the historical landscape of the times. Creators of comic books routinely wove contemporary politics into their stories, making them, for Aiken, interesting primary sources of popular culture. She has found in her classes that comic books starring superheroes offer the richest material from a historical sense and considers them to be "a surprisingly valuable window into twentieth century U.S. history." Three superheroes in particular provide insights into shifting historical contexts and themes by having mirrored developments in American culture over the course of the last seventy years. "A closer look at Captain America, Wonder Woman, and Spider-Man can enable teachers and students to examine concepts of gender, race, patriotism, and historical change through a fresh new lens," she wrote in *OAH*

*Magazine of History*, noting that the message is more important than the medium.[45]

## The Untold History of the United States

It is safe to say that packaging American history as a form of popular culture offers educators an effective way to attract young people to the subject. Americans of all ages are voracious consumers of history, a fact that middle and high school teachers should accept and hopefully embrace. *The Help*, both the novel and film, for example, were hugely popular, and functioned as a historical and user-friendly way to reflect on current race relationships. The 2012 film *Abraham Lincoln: Vampire Hunter*, based on the novel, illustrated how plastic American history could be, with this alternative telling of Honest Abe's presidency drawing in millions of young people in a way a serious biography could never do. (Steven Spielberg's *Lincoln* of the same year was also a commercial success and was nominated for a dozen Academy Awards, including one for best picture.) The 2013 film *12 Years a Slave* won the Academy Award for Best Picture, while other popular recent movies, including Lee Daniels's *The Butler* and *Selma*, also explored our troubled history of race relations. The thorny issue of race often surfaces in the more compelling-than-one-might-think PBS show *Finding Your Roots*, as Henry Louis Gates Jr. takes notable people through their family tree to demonstrate that genealogy is truly living history. Recent television series such as *Mad Men*, *Boardwalk Empire*, and *Magic City* have also made American history come alive, combining fact and fiction to make the subject interesting and relevant. While presenting in classrooms the sixteenth president as a seeker of dead people who rise each night from the grave and suck blood from the living for sustenance would likely not be a good idea, such commercial treatments of American history prove that the subject can be as exciting as any.

Serious tellings of American history also illustrate its narrative power and ability to get people's attention. Throughout his career, Oliver Stone has approached American history in a unique and compelling manner, seeing cover-ups and conspiracies wherever he looked. In 2013, Showtime aired Stone's *The Untold History of the United States* in ten parts, with a book of the same name coauthored by Peter Kuznick accompanying the series. "There is a classified America we were never meant to see," went Showtime's description of the series, a line more apt for *The X-Files* than a historical documentary. Beginning with World War I and ending with the first administration of President Barack Obama, *The Untold History of the United States* was epic in scope and, expectedly, controversial in approach. For Stone and Kuznick (a professor of history at American University), American history was essentially a fairy tale constructed and sold like any other commodity, with the fundamental message being a perverted one. It was long overdue that the myth of American exceptionalism be exposed as such, they maintained, because our schools and the mainstream media were still clinging to this false belief. Rather than pursuing a noble ideal, our nation's leaders sought (and often achieved) global supremacy, our imperialist mission not unlike that of other militaristic, colonialist powers. Dominating the world came at a heavy price, Stone and Kuznick argued—specifically, a repressive national security state still very much in force. The director of such movies as *Platoon*, *Wall Street*, *JFK*, and *Nixon* took special aim at the government's creation of the Cold War (sparked by President Harry Truman's dropping of the atomic bombs on Japan to end World War II), a decision that led to the Vietnam War and, ultimately, the mess in Afghanistan. (Joseph Stalin was portrayed more favorably in the series than Truman.)[46]

The response to *The Untold History of the United States* was profound and, as with most Stone projects, polarized. Fans loved his alternate telling of the nation's past seventy-five years, while critics had major reservations about what he and Kuznick called a "revisionist narrative." Different interpretations of the past were all well and good if they were based on evidence, pointed out one such critic, City University of New York emeritus professor (and conservative) Ronald Radosh, but manipulating and ignoring evidence was quite another. Stone and Kuznick were somehow able to similarly irritate leftist scholars such as Sean Wilentz of Princeton, who saw the documentary and book as "overloaded with ideological distortion" (and the director as "off in cuckoo land"). "This book is less a work of history than a skewed political document," he wrote in the *New York Review of Books*, the television series equally propagandist. A good number of other viewers and readers (including notable historian Douglas Brinkley), however, felt the series and book (and Stone's work in general) served an important role simply by being provocative and encouraging people to rethink what may or may not have occurred.[47] All historians are selective in their material and interpretive in their presentation, after all, making Stone not all that different from other students of the past.

Happily, there are still many histories of the United States to be told and, even better, young people who are interested in doing the telling. Every June at the University of Maryland a few thousand students gather for the finals of the annual National History Day competition, an event that has grown considerably in both numbers and stature since its inception in 1974. (President Obama awarded the program the National Humanities Medal in 2011.) For the competition six hundred thousand high school students from around the world vie at the local and state levels to reach the finals by producing papers, websites, documentaries, exhibits, and performances around a specified topic. The 2013 topic was "Turning Points in History: People, Ideas and Events," giving contestants a sizable amount of room within which to work. The competition is not a historical version of the National Spelling Bee, as judges are looking for the ability to think critically and do original research versus memorize information. "Students must learn to think analytically about material, to draw conclusions, to write and present information in creative ways," said Cathy Gorn, executive director of the program—just the kind of skills that make great historians. The real benefits of the contest are showing up in the classrooms of participants, a counterpunch of sorts to the emphasis on subjects still endorsed by No Child Left Behind (now science, technology, engineering, and math). Despite all the troubles American history has faced and continues to face, National History Day points to a positive future for the subject, a clear sign that the nation's past will indeed be remembered.[48]

# Conclusion

The enthusiasm associated with National History Day is an all-too-rare opportunity to be cautiously optimistic about where American history may be heading. It also proves that history itself can be an exciting subject of interest to young people—something many have doubted over the years, and with good reason. One has to wonder if we have collectively done a disservice to the subject by presenting it in a manner that children, adolescents, and young adults find static or inert. The politics surrounding American history certainly have not helped; our combative ideologies, fear of "wrong" ideas, and oversensitivity to interpretations about the past have drained much of the inherent intrigue from the teaching and learning of the subject. This is all too unfortunate, as our common history is one of the precious few things Americans can share in our increasingly fragmented and divisive culture. We will never all agree about what took place in the past, or why, but I think we have largely missed an infrequent (at best) chance to bring us closer together.

The passion connected to American history in popular culture continues to serve as a model for what the field as a whole can potentially represent. A book, movie, or television show about events in the nation's past may occasionally cause offense to some, but as a shared experience generally operates as a vehicle of community. This is a wonderful thing, and something the education arena should learn from. American history has too often been used as an agent of power and control rather than what it is at its best: storytelling. Without the baggage of partisanship or agendas—notably, "character building" or patriotism—American history is free to exploit its essential reason for being as a window into people's lives. Nothing is more interesting than human behavior, after all, and that is idea that we have somehow forgotten when trying to teach history.

The fundamental problem with how the subject has been treated in classrooms may be that we have typically presented it as taking place in the past. This is true, of course, but often sends a message to students that it is dead and irrelevant. As many others have noted, people of the past were very much living in the present when they did the things they did, making "history" a misnomer of sorts. Rather than looking back, in other words, we should be looking sideways, as if history was a parallel universe or different dimension alongside ours. Taking a good look at that other universe or dimension helps us better understand our own, and this is the real purpose of learning history. History informs our time and place: we need to not only say this but *show* it; history is our most valuable resource for making good decisions both now and in the future.

A cultural history of American history like this one is also a valuable resource, I believe, by offering a rich body of knowledge steeped in how we as a people have interpreted our shared past. The worth of such a collection of learnings can in fact hardly be overestimated; how any society of civilization treats its history is almost always a useful lens through which to view and understand its operative values, principles, and beliefs at any given point in time. A "longitudinal" study such as this one offers the possibility of additional insights—for example, how the cultural codes of that society changed over time. This study hopefully achieved at least a small portion of that rather grand endeavor and made some sort of contribution to our collective sense of our national heritage.

A recap of the book's major themes does indeed point to a few significant and intriguing conclusions. Based on Americans' glaring, consistent ignorance of our own history, we seem to be uneasy and uncomfortable with elements of our nation's past or possibly the whole enterprise of becoming familiar with it. Our notorious habit of staying focused on the "now" and what may soon become the now no doubt is a contributing factor for our general myopia of the past. Likewise, the very concept of history is contradictory to our beloved freedom to start our lives over or to reinvent ourselves when we feel the need. But American history has not always been a pretty story, as we increasingly learn; it is absolutely filled with shameful and painful experiences. A thorough analysis of American history will inevitability reveal the startling number of exceptions to our guiding principle that "all men are created equal" (the phrase itself can be interpreted as loaded with inequality), a revelation that many of us would simply prefer not to have. Using a psychoanalytic analogy, we could perhaps be unconsciously repressing the traumas of our past, this being an explanation for why we do not want to remember much of it. Directly confronting the truthful past could very well expose the reality that we are not as exceptional as we like to believe; such a realization is capable of dealing a serious blow to our national ego.

Another key finding is how contentious and controversial a subject American history has been over the last century. Both the parameters and substance of the field have always been up for grabs since the end of World War I, with virtually all aspects of it open for discussion and in the public domain. While this could be seen as a good thing, an example of democracy in action, it also points to how the field has been regularly used as a tool with which to further a particular ideological agenda. Unlike, say, math or English, American history has had to carry a heavy political burden, and this, too, is a reason why the subject has had a troublesome experience within the educational arena. The plasticity and mercurial nature of American history has made it vulnerable to always changing political winds, weakening its foundation. American history has served as a lightning rod for those with strong, emotional views regarding what children should and should not think about their country's past, putting it squarely in the crossfire of dogmatic partisanship and making it somewhat of a victim of what might be described as collateral damage.

American history has itself to blame for many of its current problems, however. Having marginalized groups not defined by white, Anglo-Saxon men of a certain economic status for many years, the field has been pushed—and perhaps fittingly—to the margins of our educational system. The obsession with standardized testing in public schools has taken a heavy toll on American history, with educators viewing English, math, and science as those subjects that should receive priority in terms of resources and attention. This is not just unfortunate but absurd, as it has been shown repeatedly that a familiarity with the past is arguably our best opportunity to understand the complexities of the present and the possibilities of the future. Educators of yesterday recognized this and made efforts to try to restore the teaching and learning of American history in public schools, but today there is little motivation to do so. The above subjects have been deemed those vital to creating an educated citizenship, leaving American history as an arcane, rather eccentric subject offering little real value for competing in the global economy.

Although the rise and fall of American history is a fascinating story in itself, a cultural history of the subject also presents us with the opportunity, perhaps duty, to consider why it is important that the field survives and ideally prospers in the educational landscape of the future. Why should students care about American history? How can educators teach the subject more effectively? What can be done to improve what is a bleak, if not dire situation? (American students continue to perform poorly when tested in the subject, and the field remains a battleground for special interest groups.) It is easy to find fault with the pedagogy of American history, of course, as so many critics have done over the years; it is much harder to make recommendations and find solutions.

While some critics may consider it to be a rather frivolous exercise, proposing a few ways that could potentially elevate the field is, I believe, worthwhile. The most obvious remedy would be to add American history to the list of subjects that are prioritized in standardized testing. Such a thing would require a seismic shift in how we view the value of education, however, and it is thus highly unlikely to happen. Speaking and reading the English language, being able to do at least basic arithmetic, and having a working knowledge of the physical world are currently considered essential to creating an educated public, a consensus showing few signs of breaking down in the foreseeable future. What may or may have taken place in this country in the eighteenth, nineteenth, or twentieth centuries, on the other hand, falls way down on the list of educational priorities, a conclusion compounded by school districts' jitteriness when it comes to teaching the subject. Past may indeed be prologue, but educators on national, state, and local levels understandably want to steer clear of potential politics-based land mines that may cost them their jobs.

Rather than a "top-down" or "push" strategy, then, it is a "bottom-up" or "pull" strategy that offers a better chance of reinvigorating and revitalizing the field of American history. Ideally, students should want to engage with American history rather than have the subject be forced upon them. That said, different media and experiences are needed—specifically those that kids, tweens, teens, and young adults are known to enjoy. Why are schools not using video games or graphic novels to teach the subject given that those are two of young students' media of choice? Why haven't content providers partnered with film studios to create materials that students would actually enjoy given that teens represent a huge movie-going audience? In addition, having celebrities (or even fictional characters) who are popular with young people endorse American history would go a long way toward infusing the subject with some degree of coolness, a quality it certainly does not enjoy today. There might also be American history–based webisodes that young people can view online, not unlike the ones created by marketers to engage consumers or those that networks use to attract viewers to their websites. Teens (or their parents) spend billions of dollars a year on entertainment, some of it historical in nature. There is no reason substantive, pedagogically legitimate curricula cannot be developed via media that young people actively use and enjoy. School districts have to do a better job of tapping into young people's passions with regard to technology and creativity.

The power of social media has also not been adequately applied in the field; museums, libraries, archives, and other history-oriented institutions can do a much better job connecting with young people on the Internet. Young people should be encouraged to share their visit to a historical site with friends on Facebook or send a tweet while experiencing an interesting encounter with something historical in nature. It is important to keep in mind that American history is really just stories about people, and those stories can be told in any number of ways. Whatever media are used, it is clear that the traditional teaching methods are no longer viable. The textbook wars that have so divided the field over the past few decades are now virtually irrelevant because no text, regardless of its political orientation, is likely to appeal to the typical American teenager.

All that being said, there are some reasons not to be entirely pessimistic about the future of American history in this country. History will never go away, for one thing, and there is an unlimited supply of it. New stories will always be told and, although our country is a relatively young one, there is still much to be mined or retold. We can learn much from documentary film director Ken Burns, who remains the principal gatekeeper of the nation's past, with more PBS documentaries examining interesting sites of American culture on the way. After producing films whose subjects ranged from the Brooklyn Bridge to baseball to Prohibition, Burns's next projects are histories of Jackie Robinson, Vietnam, country music, and Ernest Hemingway. "I wake the dead," he has said many times, seeing his films as opportunities to make the past come alive. Burns partially funds his projects through the Better Angels Society, a philanthropic organization dedicated to "helping tell America's stories." The society is an excellent way for donors with deep pockets to ensure Burns and other documentarians of American history will get their films made, broadcast on public television, and made available to schools across the nation via the Internet.[1] This is a perfect example of how the significant gap between American history as a thriving form of popular culture and as an ailing field of education can be bridged.

Should there be any doubt, Burns's amazing body of work is definitive proof that American history is a vital subject with broad appeal today. Actually, our interest in the past has perhaps never been stronger, a by-product of our fascination with "retro" culture. Postmodernism has made contemporary society a grab bag of times and places, making history a rich source of material to reuse and recycle. American history is particularly fertile territory, filled with people, events, and artifacts that can be rediscovered and repurposed. The recent fiftieth anniversary of the year 1964 was a bonanza for U.S. history, especially as regards the events surrounding the American "invasion" of the Beatles and the "Freedom Summer." Much more revisiting of the nation's past is no doubt in store for us over the next few years as we bump into half-century markers of the turbulent late 1960s. For better or worse, baby boomers have made sure America does not forget their coming of age between the 1950s and 1970s. "We of a certain age (the age that grips levers of power, pulls strings of purse and has the biggest mouth) can't stop reliving each moment," wrote P. J. O'Rourke in *Time* in 2014, sorry now that he himself had written too much about the 1960s.[2] Generation X is actively recovering its own historical memory from the 1980s and 1990s and, unlike boomers and the counterculture, overlaying it with a heavy dose of self-mocking and kitsch. The study of "retro" itself could be a good teaching tool in American history courses, a prime example of how history is very much alive and well.

Ironically, perhaps, it is globalization that may offer the greatest hope for the future of American history. With the exception of online or digital technology, globalization promises to transform education more than anything else, and it is an opportunity that I believe those in the field should embrace. Billions of students around the world have the chance to learn American history, something that could elevate the field to an entirely new level (and perhaps improve international relations in the process). Pop culture is our leading export, after all; most people in other countries like our movies and television shows far better than our foreign policies. As entertainment, American history functions as a sort of cultural ambassador, something education can never fully achieve but can strive for. Significant changes in the standard curricula have to be made, however, if educators in countries in Europe, Asia, and the Middle East are to treat American history as a useful and objective academic discipline rather than a propagandist ideological foil.

Such changes are, happily, already being made. More teachers in the United States are approaching American history from a global context by examining the relationship of the nation to the rest of the world. In their *Teaching American History in a Global Context*, editors Carl Guarneri and James Davis illustrated the very good reasons why educators should take such an approach. In our post-9/11 world, they convincingly argued, American students will gain a richer and more useful understanding of the nation's past when set within the framework of cultural difference and global connectedness. Traditional pedagogy relies much too heavily on an "us versus them" perspective, they and their fellow contributors suggested, with typical survey courses rooted in the classic tropes of American exceptionalism and empire building. Today and in the future, emphasizing shared historical experiences rather than our being a "city upon a hill" will better serve young people, Guarneri and Davis conclude, and it is an idea with which anyone reading a newspaper would agree.[3]

One educator in particular, Laura Emerson Talamante of California State University–Dominguez Hills, has found the value of what she calls teaching U.S. history "with an eye to the world." "As young adults in a global age beyond political alliances, students . . . came away from the course with a deeper and more nuanced understanding of national history and the complexities of what it means to be an American citizen," Talamante wrote in *The History Teacher* after trying out what she called her "big-picture analysis."[4] Scholars had been discussing the value of moving toward the internationalizing of American history for at least a couple of decades, but more educators like Talamante have recently put the idea into practice.[5] Using world history as a framework to study our nation's past served as "a rich pedagogical source for the classroom," Talamante concluded, her students gaining immeasurably from an approach grounded in multiple viewpoints.[6] Such a framework represents the future of American history, I believe, as the United States embarks on a new and different course in the remainder of the twenty-first century.

# NOTES

## INTRODUCTION

1. Useful historiographies include James M. Banner Jr., *A Century of American Historiography* (New York: Bedford/St. Martin's, 2009); Maurice G. Baxter, Robert H. Ferrell, and John E. Wiltz, *The Teaching of American History in High Schools* (Bloomington: University of Indiana Press, 1964); B. J. Bernstein, ed., *Towards a New Past: Dissenting Essays in American History* (New York: Pantheon, 1968); Marcus Cunliffe and Robin Winks, eds., *Pastmasters: Some Essays on American Historians* (New York: Harper & Row, 1969); Eric Foner, ed., *The New American History* (Philadelphia: Temple University Press, 1997); Eric Foner and Lisa McGirr, *American History Now* (Philadelphia: Temple University Press, 2011); John Higham, *History: Professional Scholarship in America* (Baltimore: Johns Hopkins University Press, 1965); John Higham, *The Reconstruction of American History* (New York: Humanities Press, 1962); Richard Hofstadter, *The Progressive Historians: Turner, Parrington, Beard* (New York: Alfred A. Knopf, 1968); Michael Kammen, ed., *The Past before Us: Contemporary Historical Writing in the United States* (Ithaca NY: Cornell University Press, 1980); Richard S. Kirkendall, ed., *The Organization of American Historians and the Writing and Teaching of American History* (New York: Oxford University Press, 2011); Michael Kraus, *The Writing of American History* (Norman: University of Oklahoma Press, 1953; Bert James Loewenberg, *American History in American Thought: Christopher Columbus to Henry Adams* (New York: Simon & Schuster, 1972); Peter Novick, *That Noble Dream: The "Objectivity Question" and the American Historical Profession* (New York: Cambridge University Press, 1988); Gary B. Nash, Charlotte Crabtree, and Ross E. Dunn, *History on Trial: Culture Wars and the Teaching of the Past* (New York: Alfred A. Knopf, 1997); Roy Rosenzweig and David Thelen, *The Presence of the Past: Popular Uses of History in American Life* (New York: Columbia University Press, 1998); David D. Van Tassel, *Recording America's Past: An Interpretation of the Development of Historical Studies in America, 1607–1884* (Chicago: University of Chicago Press, 1960);

Kyle Ward, *Not Written in Stone: Learning and Unlearning American History through 200 Years of Textbooks* (New York: New Press, 2010); Committee on American History in Schools and Colleges, *American History in Schools and Colleges: The Report of the Committee on American History in Schools and Colleges of the American Historical Association, The Mississippi Valley Historical Association, The National Council for the Social Studies* (New York: Macmillan, 1944); and Harvey Wish, *The American Historian: A Social-Intellectual History of the Writing of the American Past* (New York: Oxford University Press, 1960).

2. Edward T. Linenthal and Tom Englehardt, eds., *History Wars: The* Enola Gay *and Other Battles for the American Past* (New York: Henry Holt, 1996).

3. Gary Gerstle, *American Crucible: Race and Nation in the Twentieth Century* (Princeton NJ: Princeton University Press, 2001).

## 1. THE EPIC OF AMERICA

1. JFJ, "A 'Pure History Law,'" *American Historical Review*, July 1923, 699.

2. JFJ, "A 'Pure History Law,'" 699.

3. John B. Kennedy, "The Knights of Columbus History Movement," *Current History*, December 1921, 441–43.

4. Kennedy, "The Knights of Columbus History Movement," 443.

5. W. I. Lincoln Adams, "Right and Wrong Ways of Teaching History," *Current History*, July 1922, 550–51.

6. Julia Houston Railey, "The Book Table," *Outlook*, July 11, 1923, 383.

7. Walter Hart Blumenthal, "Should American History Be Hero-Worship?," *Current History*, March 1927, 792.

8. Blumenthal, "Should American History Be Hero-Worship?"

9. Blumenthal, "Should American History Be Hero-Worship?"

10. David Saville Muzzey, "Fathers of the Republic," *The Forum*, March 1928, 411.

11. Lyon G. Tyler, "Truth the Basic Test of History," *Current History*, February 1928, 638–39.

12. Mary E. McDowell, "Historical Heroes," *The Forum*, June 1928, 957.

13. Dana Carleton Munro, "Character Building through Truthful History," *Current History*, February 1928, 632–34.

14. Elbridge Colby, "An Army View of History Teaching in the Schools," *Current History*, February 1928, 634.

15. Colby, "An Army View of History Teaching in the Schools."

16. William Hale Thompson, "Shall We Shatter the Nation's Idols in School Histories?," *Current History*, February 1928, 625.

17. Albert Bushnell Hart, "'Treasonable' Textbooks and True Patriotism," *Current History*, February 1928, 630–32. Thompson was clearly borrowing the ideas of Charles Grant Miller who, in the early 1920s, had published a pamphlet titled

*Treason to American Tradition* that similarly attacked current textbooks. Miller was now serving as an adviser to Thompson.

18. Rupert Hughes, "Plea for Frankness in Writing History," *Current History*, February 1928, 625–30; "Illinois Bar Group Reopens Big Bill's Fight with George," *Milwaukee Journal*, April 13, 1930, 3.

19. Hughes, "Plea for Frankness in Writing History," 3.

20. James Truslow Adams, "America Faces 1933's Realities," *New York Times Magazine*, January 1, 1933, SM1; James Truslow Adams, *The Epic of America* (New York: Little, Brown, 1931).

21. Adams, "America Faces 1933's Realities," SM1.

22. James Truslow Adams, "What of 'the American Dream'?," *New York Times Magazine*, May 14, 1933, SM1.

23. H. S. Commager, "Review of *The Epic of America*, by Adams," *Books*, October 4, 1931, 1; Karl Schriftglesser, "Review of *The Epic of America*, by Adams," *Boston Transcript*, October 10, 1931, 5.

24. Allen Sinclair Will, "America, Nation of Dreamers," *New York Times*, October 4, 1931, 61.

25. Anthony Brandt, "The American Dream," *American Heritage*, April–May 1981, 24.

26. Herbert E. Bolton, "The Epic of Greater America," *American Historical Review*, April 1933, 474.

27. Bernard Fay, "An Invitation to American Historians," *Harper's*, December 1932, 20–31.

28. Dexter Perkins, "America Rewrites Her History," *Current History*, January 1932, 559–64.

29. Charles A. Beard, "That Noble Dream," *American Historical Review*, October 1935, 84, 86.

30. Franklin Delano Roosevelt, quoted in "Ancient Instances," *Time*, June 22, 1936, 17.

31. "Reciting History," *Saturday Evening Post*, October 28, 1939, 22. The acts would eventually be repealed a couple of years later after Pearl Harbor.

32. James Truslow Adams, "Forces That Make Us the United States," *New York Times*, July 13, 1941, SM8.

33. Allan Nevins, "American History for Americans," *New York Times Magazine*, May 3, 1942, SM6.

34. Nevins, "American History for Americans," SM6.

35. Nevins, "American History for Americans."

36. Nevins, "American History for Americans."

37. Nevins, "American History for Americans."

38. Nevins, "American History for Americans."

39. Nevins, "American History for Americans."

40. "De-isolationized U.S. History," *Time*, November 2, 1942, 73.
41. Henry F. Pringle, "Why Not Teach American History?," *Saturday Evening Post*, January 20, 1945, 14.
42. W. A. MacDonald, "American History Must Be Better Taught," *Saturday Evening Post*, October 9, 1943, 112.
43. Pringle, "Why Not Teach American History?," 15.
44. "Blind Date with Clio," *The Nation*, May 1, 1943, 618. It should be made clear that Progressive historians were not, as critics claimed, only interested in discrediting the nation's Founding Fathers for no worthwhile reason. While many legitimately disagreed with their findings, the fact is that Charles Beard and other Progressive historians astutely revealed the economic underpinnings of many important events and policies in U.S. history. Furthermore, Progressive history should hardly be blamed for causing students' ignorance of American history during World War II; if anything, Progressive history, by taking a critical view of the past, encouraged critical thinking, something for which its proponents should receive much credit.
45. Bernard Devoto, "The Easy Chair," *Harper's*, July 1, 1943, 129.
46. Devoto, "The Easy Chair," 132.
47. "De-isolationized U.S. History."
48. Allan Nevins, "Why We Should Know Our History," *New York Times Magazine*, April 18, 1943, SM16.
49. Nevins, "Why We Should Know Our History."
50. "History Quiz," *New York Times*, December 5, 1943, SM22.
51. Pringle, "Why Not Teach American History?"

2. E PLURIBUS UNUM
1. "The American Heritage," *School Review*, November 1947, 501. The Liberty Bell had taken a few train rides but, after being damaged (both by cracking and from souvenir hunters chipping away pieces) the practice was stopped in 1915.
2. "The American Heritage."
3. Raymond B. Fosdick, quoted in "Must Understand Our Past," *Annals of Iowa*, October 1947, 131.
4. "The Methods of Teaching History," *Annals of Iowa*, April 1949, 614–15.
5. Augustus G. Rudd, "Education for the New Social Order," *Vital Speeches of the Day*, September 1, 1948, 679–84. It is dubious that an attraction to radicalism can justly be ascribed to the "failures" of the American educational system. It is also a questionable assumption that intellectuals were really more attracted to radical politics during the Cold War. To be sure, many were during the "Red Decade" of the 1930s, but not during the late 1940s or 1950s. It would be more accurate to say that anticommunists feared that cultural elites were so inclined,

even though such fears proved to be mostly unfounded. The degree to which the Red Scare and McCarthyism targeted suspected radicals on campuses throughout the country was, however, extraordinary. Faculty members at many institutions were required to sign loyalty oaths, producing a chilling effect that narrowed the terms of academic debate and helped produce the consensus school.

6. Rudd, "Education for the New Social Order."
7. Lawrence E. Metcalf, "Anti-Communism in the Classroom: Education or Propaganda?," *The Nation*, March 10, 1962, 215–24.
8. Carl Bridenbaugh, "The Neglected First Half of American History," *American Historical Review*, April 1948, 506–17.
9. Bridenbaugh, "The Neglected First Half of American History," 511.
10. James A. Boyd, "Objectives and Methods in Teaching American History," *School Review*, November 1950, 486.
11. Tressa Banks et al., "We Tested Some Beliefs about the Biographical Method," *School Review*, March 1951, 157.
12. Banks et al., "We Tested Some Beliefs about the Biographical Method."
13. Gale W. McGee, "Early Cold Wars," *Current History*, June 1950, 353.
14. Sidney Warren, "Corruption in Politics: Before the Civil War," *Current History*, February 1952, 65–69; Sidney Warren, "Corruption in Politics: Grant-Corruption Rampant," *Current History*, April 1952, 211–15.
15. Henry Steele Commager, "'Yet the Nation Survived," *New York Times Magazine*, July 5, 1953, SM5.
16. For a brilliant study of the cultural meaning and significance of the western United States, see Henry Nash Smith's classic *Virgin Land: The American West as Symbol and Myth* (Cambridge MA: Harvard University Press, 1950).
17. Neal Gabler, *Walt Disney: The Triumph of the American Imagination* (New York: Alfred A. Knopf, 2006), 516.
18. W. Harwood Huffcut, "Are We Extracting the Excitement from the American Story?," *Saturday Evening Post*, May 18, 1957, 10.
19. Huffcut, "Are We Extracting the Excitement From the American Story?," 10.
20. Dorothy Barclay, "Making Our History Come Alive," *New York Times Magazine*, April 8, 1956, SM125.
21. George Rudisill Jr., "Homogenized History," *The Nation*, May 9, 1959, 430–33.
22. Rudisill, "Homogenized History," 433.
23. Barclay, "Making Our History Come Alive."
24. Dumas Malone, "Tapping the Wisdom of the Founding Fathers," *New York Times Magazine*, May 27, 1956, SM203.
25. Malone, "Tapping the Wisdom of the Founding Fathers," SM203.

26. John Higham, "The Cult of the American Consensus," *Commentary*, January 1, 1959, 93–100.
27. Higham, "The Cult of the American Consensus," 94.
28. Higham, "The Cult of the American Consensus," 100.
29. John Higham, "Beyond Consensus: The Historian as Moral Critic," *American Historical Review*, April 1962, 609–25.
30. Higham, "Beyond Consensus," 613.
31. John Higham, ed., *The Reconstruction of American History* (New York: Harper, 1962).
32. Staughton Lynd, "The Reconstruction of American History," *Commentary*, September 1962, 271–73.
33. Leo Marx, "The Study of Man: The American Scholar Today," *Commentary*, July 1, 1961, 48.
34. Adrienne Koch, "The Historian as Scholar," *The Nation*, November 24, 1962, 358–59.
35. Koch, "The Historian as Scholar," 360.
36. David L. Norton, "The Elders of Our Tribe," *The Nation*, February 18, 1961, 148–50.
37. Marx, "The Study of Man," 48.
38. Marx, "The Study of Man," 50.
39. Josie Lawrence, "The Techniques of Correlating Negro History with American History in the High School," *Negro History Bulletin*, March 1, 1958, 141. Lawrence's efforts illustrate that African American history did not suddenly become "trendy" with the onset of the civil rights movement; rather, it was very much an existing discipline that had been deliberately pushed to the margins. (The same can be said to be true of the contemporary study of gender, sexuality, and gay and lesbian history. Many students and members of the educated public believe these subjects to be new and fashionable, although some of these groundbreaking studies go back nearly four decades.) Within the area of African American history, the early work of W. E. B. Du Bois and Carter G. Woodson remains stunningly rich and insightful, and should be included alongside later studies in that field.
40. Charles E. Stewart, "Correcting the Image of Negroes in Textbooks," *Negro History Bulletin*, November 1, 1964, 29–30, 42–44.
41. Stewart, "Correcting the Image of Negroes in Textbooks."
42. Stewart, "Correcting the Image of Negroes in Textbooks."
43. "American Teachers Association Pushes Activity in Two Vital Areas," *Negro History Bulletin*, March 1964, 149–50.
44. "American Teachers Association Pushes Activity in Two Vital Areas."
45. Raymond Pace Alexander, "Study of Negro Blasts Racial Myths," *Negro History Bulletin*, October 1, 1964, 3; emphasis in the original.

3. E PLURIBUS CONFUSION

1. Daniel J. Boorstin, *The Americans: The National Experience* (New York: Random House, 1965).
2. John P. Diggins, "Consciousness and Ideology in American History: The Burden of Daniel J. Boorstin," *American Historical Review*, February 1971, 99–118.
3. Irwin Unger, "The 'New Left' and American History: Some Recent Trends in United States Historiography," *American Historical Review*, July 1967, 1237–63.
4. Unger, "The 'New Left' and American History."
5. "Revisionism: A New, Angry Look at the American Past," *Time*, February 2, 1970, 14–15.
6. "Revisionism."
7. Edward Pessen, "The Egalitarian Myth and the American Social Reality: Wealth, Mobility, and Equality in the 'Era of the Common Man,'" *American Historical Review*, October 1971, 989–1034.
8. William W. Freehling, "The Founding Fathers and Slavery," *American Historical Review*, February 1972, 81–93.
9. Richard Hofstadter *The Progressive Historians: Turner, Beard, Parrington* (New York: Alfred A. Knopf, 1968).
10. Daniel Boorstin, *The Americans: The Democratic Experience* (New York: Random House, 1973).
11. Roberta Balstad Miller, "Women and American History," *Women's Studies*, January 1974, 105–13.
12. Miller, "Women and American History," 108.
13. June Sochen, *Herstory: A Woman's View of American History* (New York: Alfred, 1974).
14. Jonathan Ned Katz, *Gay American History: Lesbians and Gay Men in the U.S.A.* (New York: Crowell, 1976).
15. William F. Brazziel, "Negro History in the Public Schools: Trends and Prospects," *Negro History Bulletin*, November 1, 1965, 35.
16. Brazziel, "Negro History in the Public Schools."
17. "California's Law on Negro History," *Negro History Bulletin*, February 1, 1967, 21–22.
18. Brazziel, "Negro History in the Public Schools."
19. Brazziel, "Negro History in the Public Schools."
20. Stanley Axelrod, "The Treatment of the Negro in American History School Textbooks," *Negro History Bulletin*, March 1, 1966, 135.
21. Kenneth M. Stampp et al., "The Negro in American History Textbooks," *Negro History Bulletin*, October 1, 1968, 13.
22. Stampp et al., "The Negro in American History Textbooks."

23. Mervyn M. Dymally, "The Struggle for the Inclusion of Negro History in Our Text-books . . . A California Experience," *Negro History Bulletin*, December 1, 1970, 191.

24. Sidney Fine and Gerald S. Brown, *The American Past: Conflicting Interpretations of the Great Issues* (London: Macmillan, 1970).

25. C. Vann Woodward, quoted in "Putting 'Soul" into History," *America*, May 10, 1969, 557.

26. Roy Wilkins, quoted in "Minorities in Social Studies Textbooks," *Negro History Bulletin*, November 1, 1970, 167.

27. "Civil Rights and White Textbooks," *Negro History Bulletin*, January 1, 1970, 4–5.

28. Herbert Aptheker, "Black Studies and United States History," *Negro History Bulletin*, December 1, 1971, 174.

29. Jason Berry, "The Search for Roots," *The Nation*, October 2, 1976, 314.

30. C. Vann Woodward, "The Future of the Past," *American Historical Review*, February 1970, 711, 712.

31. Woodward, "The Future of the Past."

32. Joseph H. Koch, "A Process Oriented Learning Approach to U.S. History," *Clearing House*, December 1968, 230.

33. Koch, "A Process Oriented Learning Approach to U.S. History."

34. Robert L. Dunlap, "Innovation within the Conventional School Setting," *Clearing House*, December 1970, 225.

35. Harry G. Miller, "American History: Innovating or Enervating?," *Clearing House*, April 1971, 487.

36. "The 732 Steps," *Time*, June 24, 1974, 71.

37. "Pocketful of History," *Time*, July 14, 1975.

38. Bruno Bitker, "A Way to Celebrate the Bicentennial," *American Bar Association Journal*, August 1975, 944.

39. Felix Gilbert, "Bicentennial Reflections," *Foreign Affairs*, July 1976, 644.

40. Daniel J. Boorstin, "America: Our Byproduct Nation," *Time*, June 23, 1975.

41. "July 4, 1976," special issue, *Time*, June 23, 1975.

42. John D. Rockefeller III, "Of Anniversaries and Revolutions," *Vital Speeches of the Day*, July 15, 1973, 598.

43. S. I. Hayakawa, "The Good Old Days—You Can Have Them," *Saturday Evening Post*, January–February 1974, 42.

44. Gerald R. Ford, "A Special Message from President Gerald R. Ford," *Saturday Evening Post*, July–August 1976, 132.

45. "Books for a General Introduction to the American Past," *National Review*, May 28, 1976, 551.

46. Michael Kammen, "Clio and the Changing Fashions," *American Scholar*, Summer 1975, 484–96.

47. James Razzi, *Star-Spangled Fun! Things to Make, Do and See from American History* (New York: Parents Magazine Press, 1976).

48. John W. Warner, "The Rediscovery of America," *Saturday Evening Post*, April 1977, 12, 80.

49. Warner, "The Rediscovery of America," 80. For more on the bicentennial and, more generally, the ways in which Americans from all walks of life argued— sometimes strenuously—about the nation's past, see Christopher Capozzola, "It Makes You Want to Believe in the Country," in *America in the Seventies* , ed. Beth Bailey and David Farber, 29–49 (Lawrence: University Press of Kansas, 2004); and John Bodnar, *Remaking America: Public Memory, Commemoration, and Patriotism in the Twentieth Century* (Princeton NJ: Princeton University Press, 1991).

50. L. Ethan Ellis, *40 Million Schoolbooks Can't Be Wrong: Myths in American History* (New York: Macmillan, 1975).

51. David H. Burton, ed., *American History—British Historians: A Cross Cultural Approach to the American Experience* (Chicago: Nelson-Hall, 1976). xvii.

52. "E Pluribus Confusion," *Time*, September 10, 1979.

53. Frances FitzGerald, *America Revised: History Schoolbooks in the Twentieth Century* (Boston: Little, Brown, 1979).

54. William Appleman Williams, "You Aren't Lost until You Don't Know Where You've Been," *The Nation*, October 27, 1979, 406.

55. John Pare, "How the Cold War Is Taught," *Educational Leadership*, December 1979, 271–72.

56. "Was Robin Just a Hood? A Team of Texan Critics Take Textbooks to Task," *Time*, December 31, 1979. Another especially interesting "textbook war" took place in Kanawha County, West Virginia, between 1974 and 1975; the dramatic event, which spilled over into the public arena, illuminated the extent to which parental concerns about the harm "revisionist" history could allegedly do to kids.

4. THE FALL OF THE AMERICAN ADAM

1. Howard Zinn, *A People's History of the United States* (New York: Harper & Row, 1980).

2. C. Vann Woodward, "The Fall of the American Adam," *New Republic*, December 2, 1981, 13–16.

3. Daniel J. Elazar, "Meaning of the Seventies," *Society*, January–February 1980, 7–11.

4. Amitai Etzioni, "Rehashing the Seventies," *Society*, January–February 1980, 13.

5. Woodward, "The Fall of the American Adam," 14.

6. Woodward, "The Fall of the American Adam," 14.

7. John A. Garraty, "What's Happening in History," *American Heritage*, October–November 1983, 8–9.

8. Thomas Bender, "Making History Whole Again," *New York Times Book Review*, October 6, 1985, 42.

9. Herbert G. Gutman, "Whatever Happened to History?," *The Nation*, November 21, 1981, 554.

10. Carl Degler, "Forum: Carl Degler Asks 'Can the American Past Be Put Back Together Again?,'" *History Today*, August 1983, 3–4.

11. Degler, "Forum," 4.

12. "Teach Social and Political Values Through Study of History: Bennett," *Phi Delta Kappan*, June 1985, 738.

13. Lillian Stewart Carl, "It Was 'Gorilla' Warfare to Some Students," *Smithsonian Magazine*, June 1982, 156.

14. Jane Ingram, Kenneth T. Henson, and Adolph B. Crew, "American Studies at Central High," *Phi Delta Kappan*, December 1984, 296–97.

15. Diane Ravitch, "Decline and Fall of Teaching History," *New York Times Magazine*, November 17, 1985, 50–54.

16. Ravitch, "Decline and Fall of Teaching History," 50.

17. Ravitch, "Decline and Fall of Teaching History," 51.

18. Lucia Solorzano, "Bridging the 'History Gap': New Challenge for U.S. Schools," *U.S. News & World Report*, November 18, 1985, 81.

19. Solorzano, "Bridging the 'History Gap.'"

20. Diane Ravitch and Chester E. Finn Jr., *What Do Our 17-Year Olds Know? A Report on the First National Assessment of History and Literature* (New York: HarperCollins, 1989).

21. Ravitch and Finn, quoted in Margo Hammond, "Education's Hottest Issue: What You Should Know," *Scholastic Update*, November 6, 1987, 3.

22. Peter J. Parish, "American History Arrives in Europe," *New York Times Book Review*, February 3, 1985, 28–29.

23. Eileen M. Gardner, "Teaching History in the U.S. and USSR," *Education Digest*, October 1988, 29–32.

24. David K. Shipler, "How We See Each Other: The View from America," *New York Times Magazine*, November 10, 1985, SM34–SM40.

25. Gilbert Sewall, "American History Textbooks: Their Literary Merit," *Education Digest*, October 1988, 23.

26. Gilbert T. Sewall, "American History Textbooks: Where Do We Go from Here?," *Phi Delta Kappan*, April 1988, 553.

27. Sewall, "American History Textbooks."

28. Jeffrey L. Pasley, "Not-So-Good Books," *New Republic*, April 27, 1987, 20–22.

29. Barbara Vobejda, "Why Censor Religion?," *Current*, October 1987, 30–32.

30. William Broyles Jr., "A Celebration of America," *Newsweek*, Special Issue (Spring 1983), 10; Ronald Steel, "Life in the Last Fifty Years," *Esquire*, June 1983, 23.

31. Paul A. Fideler, "Have Historians Lost Their Perspective on the Past at the Expense of the Future?," *Change*, January–February 1984, 7–9.

32. Fideler, "Have Historians Lost Their Perspective on the Past?," 7.

33. Fideler, "Have Historians Lost Their Perspective on the Past?"

34. Bernard A. Weisberger, "American History Is Falling Down," *American Heritage*, February–March 1987, 27.

35. Weisberger, "American History Is Falling Down."

36. Weisberger, "American History Is Falling Down."

37. Paul Gagnon, "Why Study History?," *Atlantic Monthly*, November 1988, 43.

38. Gagnon, "Why Study History?"

39. Gagnon, "Why Study History?"

40. Connie Quinlivan, "Expeditions to the O.K. Corral," *Newsweek*, May 10, 1988, 10.

41. Samuel S. Wineburg and Suzanne M. Wilson, "Models of Wisdom in the Teaching of History," *Phi Delta Kappan*, September 1988, 50–58.

42. Wineburg and Wilson, "Models of Wisdom in the Teaching of History."

43. Wineburg and Wilson, "Models of Wisdom in the Teaching of History," 56.

44. "Remember Me Not," *Phi Delta Kappan*, January 1989, 407–8.

45. "Farewell and Hail," *National Review*, February 10, 1989, 11.

46. "Reagan and Historical Memory," *National Review*, February 10, 1989, 11–12.

47. Ronald Reagan, quoted in "Reagan and Historical Memory," 12.

48. Michael Kazin, "The New Historians Recapture the Flag," *New York Times Book Review*, July 2, 1989, 1, 19, 21.

49. Dave Barry, *Dave Barry Slept Here: A Sort of History of the United States* (New York: Random House, 1989), x.

5. WE THE PEOPLES

1. John Fonte, "We the Peoples," *National Review*, March 25, 1996, 47.

2. Fonte, "We the Peoples," 47.

3. Lewis Lord and Jeannye Thornton, "1940 America," *U.S. News & World Report*, August 27–September 3, 1990, 44.

4. Gerald Parshall, "The Face of Victory," *U.S. News & World Report*, December 2, 1991, 52.

5. Dan B. Fleming and Burton I. Kaufman, "The Forgotten War: Korea," *Education Digest*, December 1990, 71–72.

6. Timothy Jacobson, "America Needs Its History—Today!," *History Today*, March 1991, 9.

7. Meg Greenfield, "Buy—And Read with Care," *Newsweek*, June 10, 1991, 68.

8. Michael Kimmelman, "Old West, New Twist at the Smithsonian," *New York Times*, May 26, 1991, 1, 27.

9. Bernard A. Weisberger, "Staking a Claim on the Past," *American Heritage,* October 1991, 22.

10. Weisberger, "Staking a Claim on the Past," 22.

11. Arthur Schlesinger Jr., *The Disuniting of America: Reflections on a Multicultural Society* (New York: W. W. Norton, 1992).

12. Martha Saxton, "The New History: Showing Children the Dark Side," *New York Times Book Review,* November 13, 1994, 32.

13. Saxton, "The New History."

14. Alexander Stille, "The Betrayal of History," *New York Review of Books,* June 11, 1998, 15–20.

15. P. Boyer, *Todd & Curti's The American Nation* (New York: Harcourt School, 1994).

16. John Leo, "Affirmative Action History," *U.S. News & World Report,* March 2, 1994, 24.

17. Jon Wiener, "History Lesson," *New Republic,* January 2, 1995, 9.

18. LynNell Hancock and Nina Archer Biddle, "Red, White, and Blue," *Newsweek,* November 7, 1994, 54.

19. Eric Foner, "Bobbing History," *The Nation,* September 25, 1995, 302.

20. Wiener, "History Lesson," 9.

21. John Leo, "History Standards Are Bunk," *U.S. News & World Report,* February 6, 1995, 23.

22. John Leo, "The Hijacking of American History," *U.S. News & World Report,* November 14, 1994, 36.

23. Eric Alterman, "Culture Wars," *Rolling Stone,* October 19, 1995, 45.

24. Reo Christenson, "Real Patriots Learn Real History," *Christianity Today,* November 5, 1990, 12.

25. Michael Kammen, "History as a Lightning Rod," OAH *Newsletter,* May 1995, 1, 6.

26. LynNell Hancock and Nina Biddle, "History Lessons," *Newsweek,* July 10, 1995, 28.

27. "Makeup Test: More History, Less P.C.," *Newsweek,* April 15, 1996, 67.

28. Herbert London, "National Standards for History Judged Again," *Society,* January–February 1997, 28.

29. LynNell Hancock and Pat Wingert, "A Mixed Report Card," *Newsweek,* November 13, 1995, 69.

30. Lewis H. Lapham, "Time Lines," *Harper's,* January 1996, 7.

31. David B. Danbom, "Learning Lessons from History," USA *Today Magazine,* September 1999, 30.

32. Douglas Brinkley, "Caution: I Brake for History," *American Heritage,* April 1996, 62.

33. Robert Adams, "Smithsonian Horizons," *Smithsonian,* February 1994, 8.

34. Jon Wiener, "Tall Tales and True," *The Nation,* January 31, 1994, 133–35.

35. Wiener, "Tall Tales and True," 134.
36. Adams, "Smithsonian Horizons," 8.
37. I. Michael Heyman, "Smithsonian Perspectives," *Smithsonian*, July 1995, 10.
38. "America's Attic," *USA Today Magazine*, July 1996, 20–29.
39. I. Michael Heyman, "Smithsonian Perspectives," *Smithsonian*, March 1997, 14.
40. Heyman, "Smithsonian Perspectives," 14.
41. John Patrick Diggins, "Can the Social Historian Get It Right?," *Society*, January–February 1997, 9–19.
42. Stille, "The Betrayal of History."
43. Stapley W. Emberling and Gilbert T. Sewall, "A New Generation of History Textbooks," *Current*, February 1999, 31.
44. Gerald F. Kreyche, "American Masters Malign Our Nation," *USA Today Magazine*, January 1999, 82.
45. Emberling and Sewall, "A New Generation of History Textbooks."
46. William Cronon et al., "Teaching American History," *American Scholar*, Winter 1998, 91–106.
47. Cronon et al., "Teaching American History," 92.
48. Christopher Hitchens, "Goodbye to All That: Why Americans Are Not Taught History," *Harper's*, November 1998, 37.
49. Roger Mudd, "There Isn't Any Such Thing as the Past," *American Heritage*, February–March 1999, 114–25.
50. Roy Rosenzweig and David Thelen, *The Presence of the Past: The Meaning of History in American Life* (New York: Columbia University Press, 1998).
51. Rosenzweig and Thelen, *The Presence of the Past*.

6. THE FRAY OF HISTORY

1. Stephen Bertman, "America Is Suffering from Cultural Amnesia," *USA Today*, November 2001, 18–19.
2. Wilfred M. McClay, "History for a Democracy," *Wilson Quarterly*, Autumn 2001, 99.
3. Bertman, "America Is Suffering from Cultural Amnesia," 18.
4. Bertman, "America Is Suffering from Cultural Amnesia."
5. Bruce Cole, "The Urgency of Memory," *Vital Speeches of the Day*, July 1, 2002, 565.
6. Joshua Zeitz, "Are Our Liberties in Peril?," *American Heritage*, December 2001, 32.
7. Roger Rosenblatt, "Back into the Fray of History," *Time*, November 12, 2001, 106.
8. Nathan Ward, "The Fire Last Time," *American Heritage*, December 2001, 46.
9. Eric Foner, "Changing History," *The Nation*, September 23, 2002, 5–6.
10. Robert J. Samuelson, "Democracy in America," *Newsweek*, November 13, 2000, 61.

11. Michael Barone, "A Place Like No Other," *U.S. News & World Report*, June 28, 2004, 38–39.
12. McClay, "History for a Democracy," 99.
13. McClay, "History for a Democracy," 99.
14. Theodore K. Rabb, "'No Child' Left Behind Historical Literacy," *Education Digest*, October 2004, 18–21.
15. Rabb, "'No Child' Left Behind Historical Literacy." 20.
16. James A. Bryant Jr., "Using History to Save Our Nation," *Education Digest*, November 2005, 25–28.
17. R. Emmett Tyrrell Jr., "Coogler Laureate 2004," *American Spectator*, March 2005, 67.
18. Ann Hulbert, "Textbook Message," *New York Times Magazine*, February 6, 2005, 13.
19. Alex Stein, "The Teaching American History Program: An Introduction and Overview," *History Teacher*, February 2003, 178–85.
20. Diane Ravitch, "Commentary on the Results of the 2001 National Assessment of Educational Progress in U.S. History," press release, U.S. Department of Education, Washington DC, May 2002.
21. Stein, "The Teaching American History Program," 185.
22. Stan Pesick and Shelley Weintraub, "DeTocqueville's Ghost: Examining the Struggle for Democracy in America," *History Teacher*, February 2003, 231–51.
23. Sema Brainin, "Equity, Excellence, and Engagement of Everyone in United States History," *OAH Magazine of History*, January 2004, 59–62.
24. Rachel G. Ragland, "Changing Secondary Teachers' Views of Teaching American History," *History Teacher*, February 2007, 219–46.
25. James W. Loewen, "Book Reviews," *Journal of American History*, September 2010, 481–82; Mary Lopez and Robert D. Johnston, "Reviews," *History Teacher*, May 2011, 470–72.
26. Wilson J. Warren, "Closing the Distance between Authentic History Pedagogy and Everyday Classroom Practice," *History Teacher*, February 2007, 250–55.
27. David J. Voelker, "Assessing Student Understanding in Introductory Courses: A Sample Strategy," *History Teacher*, August 2008, 505–18.
28. Schaun Wheeler, "History Is Written by the Learners: How Student Views Trump United States History Curricula," *History Teacher*, November 2007, 12.
29. Kevin St. Jarre, "Reinventing Social Studies," *Phi Delta Kappan*, May 2008, 650.
30. Robert B. Bain, "A Bad Argument for a Reasonable Position," *Phi Delta Kappan*, May 2008, 654–59.
31. David McCullough, "History and Knowing Who We Are," *American Heritage*, Winter 2008, 14.

32. McCullough, "History and Knowing Who We Are," 17.

33. Andrew Curry, "The Better Angels," *U.S. News & World Report*, September 30, 2002, 56.

34. Joan Richardson, "Lies and American History," *Phi Delta Kappan*, April 2010, 17–22.

35. James W. Loewen, *Teaching What Really Happened: How to Avoid the Tyranny of Textbooks and Get Students Excited about Doing History* (New York: Teachers College Press, 2009).

36. Mariah Blake, "Revisionaries," *Washington Monthly*, January–February 2010, 13–18.

37. Jim Hightower, "No Enlightenment in Texas," *Progressive*, May 2010, 46.

38. Don McLeroy, quoted in Evan Smith, "The Texas Curriculum Massacre," *Newsweek*, April 26, 2010, 34.

39. Blake, "Revisionaries."

40. "Don't Know Much about History," *Christian Century*, July 12, 2011, 7.

41. "Don't Know Much about History."

42. "Don't Know Much about History."

43. Niall Ferguson, "How to Get Smart Again," *Newsweek*, March 28, 2011, 62–63.

44. Ferguson, "How to Get Smart Again," 63.

45. Katherine G. Aiken, "Superhero History: Using Comic Books to Teach U.S. History," *OAH Magazine of History*, April 2010, 47.

46. Andrew Goldman, "His History," *New York Times Magazine*, November 25, 2012, SM22; Sean Wilentz, "Cherry-Picking Our History," *New York Review of Books*, February 21, 2013, 14.

47. Goldman, "His History"; Wilentz, "Cherry-Picking Our History," 14.

48. Cathy Gorn, quoted in Richard Ensberger, "National History Day Lets Students Shine," *American History*, August 2013, 9.

CONCLUSION

1. Thebetterangelssociety.org.

2. P. J. O'Rourke, "Keeping the '60s on Life Support," *Time*, January 13, 2014.

3. Wayne Journell, "Teaching American History in a Global Context," *The History Teacher*, August 2009, 516–17; Carl Guarneri and James Davis, *Teaching American History in a Global Context* (Armonk NY: M. E. Sharpe, 2008).

4. Laura Emerson Talamante, "Teaching United States History with an Eye to the World," *The History Teacher*, May 2008, 392.

5. See, for example, David Thelen, "Of Audiences, Borderlands, and Comparisons: Toward the Internationalization of American History," *Journal of American History*, September 1992, 432–62.

6. Talamante, "Teaching United States History with an Eye to the World," 397.

# SELECTED BIBLIOGRAPHY

Adams, James Truslow. *The Epic of America*. New York: Little, Brown, 1931.

Bailey, Beth, and David Farber. *America in the Seventies*. Lawrence: University Press of Kansas, 2004.

Barry, Dave. *Dave Barry Slept Here: A Sort of History of the United States*. New York: Random House, 1989.

Beard, Charles A. *An Economic Interpretation of the Constitution of the United States*. New York: Macmillan, 1913.

Bodnar, John. *Remaking America: Public Memory, Commemoration, and Patriotism in the Twentieth Century*. Princeton NJ: Princeton University Press, 1991.

Boorstin, Daniel J. *The Americans: The Colonial Experience*. New York: Random House, 1958.

———. *The Americans: The Democratic Experience*. New York: Random House, 1973.

———. *The Americans: The National Experience*. New York: Random House, 1965.

Brokaw, Tom. *The Greatest Generation*. New York: Random House, 1998.

Burton, David H., ed. *American History—British Historians: A Cross Cultural Approach to the American Experience*. Chicago: Nelson-Hall, 1976.

Cooke, Alistair. *Alistaire Cooke's America*. New York: Alfred A. Knopf, 1973.

Cronon, William. *Changes in the Land: Indians, Colonists, and the Ecology of New England*. New York: Hill & Wang, 1983.

Davis, Kenneth C. *Don't Know Much about History: Everything You Need to Know about American History but Never Learned*. New York: Crown, 1990.

Ellis, L. Ethan. *40 Million Schoolbooks Can't Be Wrong: Myths in American History*. New York: Macmillan, 1975.

Fine, Sidney, and Gerald S. Brown. *The American Past: Conflicting Interpretations of the Great Issues*. London: Macmillan, 1970.

Fink, Leon. *Workingmen's Democracy: The Knights of Labor and American Politics*. Urbana: University of Illinois Press, 1983.

FitzGerald, Frances. *America Revised: History Schoolbooks in the Twentieth Century.* Boston: Little, Brown, 1979.

Gabler, Neal. *Walt Disney: The Triumph of the American Imagination.* New York: Alfred A. Knopf, 2006.

Gerstle, Gary. *American Crucible: Race and Nation in the Twentieth Century.* Princeton NJ: Princeton University Press, 2001.

———. *Working-Class Americanism: The Politics of Labor in a Textile City, 1914–1960.* New York: Cambridge University Press, 1989.

Gladwell, Malcolm. *The Tipping Point: How Little Things Can Make a Big Difference.* New York: Little, Brown, 2000.

Goodwin, Doris Kearns. *No Ordinary Time: Franklin and Eleanor Roosevelt: The Home Front in World War II.* New York: Simon & Schuster, 1995.

Guarneri, Carl, and James Davis. *Teaching American History in a Global Context.* Armonk NY: M. E. Sharpe, 2008.

Hakim, Joy. *A History of Us.* New York: Oxford University Press, 1993.

Haley, Alex. *Roots: The Saga of an American Family.* New York: Doubleday, 1976.

Higham, John. *The Reconstruction of American History.* New York: Humanities Press, 1962.

Hofstadter, Richard. *The Progressive Historians: Turner, Parrington, Beard.* New York: Alfred A. Knopf, 1968.

Katz, Jonathan Ned. *Gay American History: Lesbians and Gay Men in the U.S.A.* New York: Crowell, 1976.

Linenthal, Edward T., and Tom Englehardt, eds. *History Wars: The Enola Gay and Other Battles for the American Past.* New York: Henry Holt, 1996.

Loewen, James W. *Lies My Teacher Told Me: Everything Your American History Textbook Got Wrong.* New York: New Press, 2008.

———. *Teaching What Really Happened: How to Avoid the Tyranny of Textbooks and Get Students Excited about Doing History.* New York: Teachers College Press, 2009.

Lukacs, John. *The Future of History.* New Haven CT: Yale University Press, 2012.

McCullough, David. *John Adams.* New York: Simon & Schuster, 2001.

———. *1776.* New York: Simon & Schuster, 2005.

———. *Truman.* New York: Simon & Schuster, 1992.

Morrison, Toni. *Beloved.* New York: Alfred A. Knopf, 1987.

Potter, David M. *People of Plenty: Economic Abundance and the American Character.* Chicago: University of Chicago Press, 1954.

Ragland, Rachel G., and Kelly A. Woestman, eds. *The Teaching American History Project: Lessons for Educators and Historians.* New York: Routledge, 2009.

Ravitch, Diane, and Chester E. Finn Jr. *What Do Our 17-Year-Olds Know?* New York: HarperCollins, 1988.

Razzi, James. *Star-Spangled Fun! Things to Make, Do and See from American History.* New York: Parents Magazine Press, 1976.

Rosenzweig, Roy, and David Thelen. *The Presence of the Past: The Meaning of History in American Life.* New York: Columbia University Press, 1998.

Roth, Philip. *The Plot against America.* New York: Houghton Mifflin, 2004.

Schlesinger, Arthur M. *New Viewpoints in American History.* New York: Macmillan, 1922.

Schlesinger, Arthur M., Jr. *The Disuniting of America: Reflections on a Multicultural Society.* New York: W. W. Norton, 1992.

Smith, Henry Nash. *Virgin Land: The American West as Symbol and Myth.* Cambridge MA: Harvard University Press, 1950.

Sochen, June. *Herstory: A Woman's View of American History.* New York: Alfred, 1974.

Stewart, Jon, and the Writers of the Daily Show. *America (the Book): Teacher's Edition: A Citizen's Guide to Democracy Inaction.* New York: Grand Central, 2006.

Stone, Oliver, and Peter Kuznick. *The Untold History of the United States.* New York: Gallery Books, 2012.

Styron, William. *The Confessions of Nat Turner.* New York: Random House, 1967.

Vidal, Gore. *Burr.* London: William Heinemann, 1974.

Walker, Alice. *The Color Purple.* New York: Harcourt, Brace, 1982.

Wilentz, Sean. *Chants Democratic: New York City and the Rise of the American Working Class, 1788–1850.* New York: Oxford University Press, 1984.

Woods, Thomas. *The Politically Incorrect Guide to American History.* Washington DC: Regnery, 2006.

Zinn, Howard. *A People's History of the United States.* New York: Harper & Row, 1980.

CPSIA information can be obtained at www.ICGtesting.com
Printed in the USA
LVOW07*2108040915

452890LV00010BA/40/P